THE SPIRITUALITY OF SEX

THE SPIRITUALITY
OF SEX

J. Harold Ellens

Foreword by Donald Capps

Psychology, Religion, and Spirituality

Westport, Connecticut
London

Library of Congress Cataloging-in-Publication Data

Ellens, J. Harold, 1932–
    The spirituality of sex / J. Harold Ellens ; foreword by Donald Capps.
        p.   cm. — (Psychology, religion, and spirituality, ISSN 1546–8070)
    Includes bibliographical references and index.
    ISBN 978–0–313–36261–3 (alk. paper)
    1. Sex—Religious aspects—Christianity.   I. Title.
    BT708.E39   2009
    233'.5—dc22   2008051409

British Library Cataloguing in Publication Data is available.

Library of Congress Catalog Card Number: 2008051409
ISBN: 978–0–313–36261–3
ISSN: 1546–8070

First published in 2009

Praeger Publishers, 88 Post Road West, Westport, CT 06881
An imprint of Greenwood Publishing Group, Inc.
www.praeger.com

Printed in the United States of America

The paper used in this book complies with the
Permanent Paper Standard issued by the National
Information Standards Organization (Z39.48–1984).

10 9 8 7 6 5 4 3 2 1

To all true lovers
Past, present, and future
Who wish to be really present
To their beloved
In the moments of play and ecstasy;
And who are willing
To do the hard work of learning
All the valid techniques of
Tenderness and attention!

To Abelard and Heloise,
The ultimate symbols of daring
And authentic love;
And all the blessed and forlorn
For whom they stand:
What was, what can be,
Or might have been.

There are those who constantly
Walk away from you.
Let them go.
They are a violation
Of the very essence
Of life's vital force:
The spirituality of sex.

Some say sometimes that
"Good guys always stay too long!"
In my seasons of lost love
I am quite sure that I am right
In seizing upon that sentiment.
But a moment of gentle kindness,
If turned my way,
Is a moment when I feel anguish
That the slogan is just an angry lie!

To all true lovers
Whose enduring devotion
Has won out
In the end!

CONTENTS

Contents

FOREWORD

When students approach me with questions about sexuality, I instinctively refer them to my colleague, Robert Dykstra, who teaches our courses on sexuality at Princeton Theological Seminary. When I assigned my own book, *A Time to Laugh*, in a class, I pointed out the model of the person depicted in a rather crude drawing of my own, a "self-portrait," and noted that it located the self-center in the brain, the spirit-center in the heart, and the soul-center in the liver.[1] I suggested to the class that there was something missing in this picture because it ended at the waist: "There's no sex-center!" I suggested that if anyone wanted to learn about the fourth center of the person, they should take a course from my colleague, Robert Dykstra.

When J. Harold Ellens asked me to write this foreword, my initial instinct was to suggest that he get my colleague, Robert Dykstra. He is a lot more interested in sex than I am. But then I began to feel a quiver in my liver, which told me that it was time to do a bit of *soul*-searching: Why do I wish to hold the topic of sex at arm's length? Why do I focus on organs above the waist and leave those below the waist to others?

So I agreed to write this foreword. I rationalized my agreement on the grounds that there must be others out there who might feel the same as I do about the subject. Maybe, I thought, a foreword written by someone such as I would actually serve the interests of the author and publisher in ways that a foreword by someone who has an easy familiarity with the topic would not. My *self*-center in the brain found this argument relatively persuasive, and my *spirit*-center in the heart got on board with it too, so before long all three of me were of one accord.

Then I began reading *The Spirituality of Sex* and came to the realization that this book, although written for many others, was written for me. I especially sensed this when I read and reflected on Ellens's imaginative idea that all the readers of this book might gather in a classroom somewhere sometime. The imagined class of readers would, of course, be very large, so large in fact that I could slip in rather easily and not be noticed. Then, however, the teacher-guide, Ellens himself, would begin to get personal. We would be asked to describe a portrait of a marriage or love relationship that expressed the authentic psycho-spirituality of communion, union, ecstasy, and eternity and then to compare this picture with the reality of our lives: "What would your picture look like? How would that compare with your experience and your expectation for your own love relationships? Would the two pictures be similar? Would they have anything to do with the overshadowing meaning of the *spirituality of sex*, as indicated in the title of this book and described in our discussion?" No doubt, we would all feel a bit exposed. Some of us would raise our hands to be recognized, but others of us would shuffle our feet or look furtively at the door, wondering if anyone would notice if we quietly slipped out.

As I thought of myself as a member of that class, I felt a bit like the child in preschool who, while drawing a picture, looks anxiously at what the other children are drawing. Just as he is about to scrap his own effort, the teacher says, "Let the picture be what *you* want it to be." What I especially appreciate about this book is that it does not present an ideal picture of the spirituality of sex, one to which all of us are encouraged to aspire. At the same time, it provides a wonderful array of cases, of individuals and couples, who are struggling to discover what it is that they *do* expect from their love relationships and how the two pictures, actual and ideal, might more closely resemble one another. I relished these cases because they avoided caricature and instead presented these individuals and couples as thoughtful yet perplexed, struggling yet hopeful, and above all as persons whose desires are often more profound and heartfelt than their surface behaviors tend to convey.

I was also inspired by the way in which two biblical pictures were juxtaposed to one another: the affirmation of our sexual natures in the story of Adam and Eve and the denigration of our sexual natures in Paul's hierarchical understanding of the human person. Paul, unfortunately, suggests that our spiritual nature reflects our higher aspirations, and our sexual nature reflects our degraded passions. The very title of this book, *The Spirituality of Sex*, challenges this unfortunate, even pernicious distinction. By challenging it, however, Ellens is able to explore a problem that Paul was unable to consider, the fact that so many persons today settle for so little as far as their sexual natures are concerned.

Ellens's phrase "sexual gymnastics" is a wonderful term for these low expectations. It brings to mind Stephen Dunn's poem titled "Decorum." It is about a class discussion of a student's poem that contained the line, "They were making love up against the gymnasium wall."[2] Members of Dunn's class argued that the student writer should call what they were doing by its proper name—that is, "fucking." Dunn says that he found himself leaning toward those who favored that expression because they were personally funnier and seemed to have more experience with the happy varieties of the subject. But one of the male students said he did not think there was any difference between that and "making love." After all, "you fuck 'em and you call it love; you tell 'em what they want to hear." The class jeered, and another male student told him that he was the kind of guy "who gives fucking a bad name."

This discussion went on until Dunn felt it was time to intervene. He said that he usually disliked that word in a poem but thought that maybe in this case it might be right. He really was not sure. Dunn noticed a tear form and fall down the cheek of the woman who had written that line. Clearly, the poem was about her personally. Dunn said quickly that there was one thing of which he *was* quite certain, namely, that the word "gymnasium" was the wrong choice because it made the act seem too public, more vulgar than she wanted it to be: "How about 'boat house'?" he suggested. Authentic sexual experience is about emotional and spiritual intimacy, Ellens points out forcefully.

The phrase "sexual gymnastics" also reminded me of the experience of a pastor I knew. A woman who had been attending his church told the church council that he and she had had sexual relations in the backseat of his Volkswagen. He rebutted her claims on the grounds that someone as fat as he had trouble enough getting into the backseat of his car, much less performing the "sexual gymnastics" of which he had been accused.

I especially appreciated the fact that J. Harold Ellens, well known for his knowledge of the Bible, made certain that a third biblical image would be placed, as it were, between the picture of Adam and Eve and their desiring of one another and the picture of Paul frowning on his "lower" nature. This is the image of sexuality portrayed in the Song of Solomon, known also as the Song of Songs. As Ellens shows, the way in which this book of the Bible builds to a climax, followed by peace and tranquility, reflects the chemistry of sex itself. His reflections on the Song of Solomon occur in the chapter on the spirituality of wooing and courting. Once introduced, however, this lovely poem hovers over the book as a whole, a steady reminder of the fact that wooing and courting remain a central feature of all authentic love relationships. The author and I can testify to the truth of this claim because we are both older men. This being so, perhaps readers of this foreword will forgive a personal testimony that reflects, I believe, the essential spirit of *The Spirituality of Sex:*

One evening while I was reading *The Norton Book of Light Verse*, I came across the following poem by James B. Naylor:[3]

Authorship
King David and King Solomon
Led merry, merry lives,
With many, many lady friends
And many, many wives.

But when old age crept over them,
With many, many qualms,
King Solomon wrote the Proverbs
And King David wrote the Psalms.

I grudgingly admitted to myself that Naylor's poem was clever, but because I was struggling with old age creeping over me, I set to work on a poem of dissent. Between the two kings, I felt that my best case would be Solomon. Here's what I wrote:

The Canonical King
Solomon wrote his Proverbs
As a young precocious sage,
Then penned Ecclesiastes
In cynical middle age.
But old age brought him wisdom
Which inspired Songs on Sex.
And this concludes my lecture
On the works of Solomon Rex.

Courageous, even defiant words, no doubt, but were they true? I admitted that one could read the Song of Solomon as a poem about young love. After all, as indicated by the citations from the Song of Solomon in *The Spirituality of Sex*, the woman views her beloved as like "a gazelle or a young stag," and at one point she asks him, point blank, if he would try to be like "a young stag upon the mountains."

As Ellens points out, however, these are *metaphors* of longing and desire, and because they are metaphors, there is no reason for us to assume that the Song of Solomon has to do only with lovers who are in the vigor of their youth. On the contrary, as Ellens puts it, this "litany of love" sets forth "the Bible's model of ideal joy and the spirituality of sex," and this being the case, it would be strange indeed if this model were restricted to the young, as if we are to assume that at some unspecified age we are meant to relinquish the Bible's model and adopt some lesser model of relating.

To prove my theory that Song of Solomon is the work of an older man, I clambered into bed one night and said to my wife (quoting from Song of Solomon 6:6): "Your teeth are like a flock of ewes, that have come up from the washing; all of them bear twins, and not one among them is bereaved."

"You say such sweet nothings," she murmured, and as she snuggled into my arms, I imagined that she was thinking to herself, "I am my beloved's, and his desire is for me" (7:10). As I lay there, these words came floating through the open window: "The flowers appear on the earth: the time of singing has come, and the voice of the turtledove is heard in our land" (2:12). As the dictionary points out, the turtledove is "any of several Old World wild doves noted for their plaintive cooing, and the affection that the mates are traditionally thought of as showing toward each other."[4] It occurred to me that the two of us are "old World" alright, but we are also "wild doves," and what others may hear through the open window as tremulous snoring sounds are, to us, the melodious trill of plaintive cooing.

I may be forgiven, therefore, for saying that my favorite chapter of *The Spirituality of Sex* is chapter 8, "Tenderness: The Continued Cherishing." I was moved by Ellens's observation that it is a very common experience in clinical work to have a patient say that he or she is in a relationship in which there is very little cherishing and only the mechanics of sex. There is no real union and communion. He says that such persons often insist that what they really miss is someone holding them. I was also convinced, as if I needed any convincing, that he is absolutely right when he says in this regard that men and women need to make clear what it is that they really desire and long for. It is not good for one to entice the other into sexual intercourse if one's real desire is to be held or cuddled. As the poet William Stafford says in "A Ritual to Read to Each Other," "The signals we give, yes or no, or maybe, should be clear" because "the darkness around us is deep."[5]

J. Harold Ellens has given us a brilliant, informative, and above all, invitational series of lessons, as it were, on the spirituality of sex. If he were to hold a class of all his readers, some of us might hesitate to get so sexually personal and so spiritually intimate as Ellens does in this book. You may say to yourself, "Sex is not my thing" or "Spirituality is not my thing" or the "Spirituality *of* sex is not my thing." It's not my place to say that you would be wrong to go off in search of someone talking about violence instead. It *is* my place, however, to say that in this book you will find yourself sharing with its author many knowing smiles and insightful nods of recognition of experiences you never felt you could read or talk about. Perhaps, like the young woman in Stephen Dunn's poem, you will find a tear trickling down your cheek as you sense that J. Harold Ellens knows what you have been trying to say all this time—and has now given you the words to say it.

Donald Capps

PREFACE

The two most important aspects of human life are our spirituality and sexuality. *The Spirituality of Sex* describes the psychological and spiritual facts of life. That is, this book discusses in detail the way in which sexuality shows up in all aspects of our lives and influences them all. The energy that is generated by our sexual drives is the dynamic source of all the forces that shape our experience. It shapes our life, our motives, and our thoughts. It forms our feelings, desires, and spiritual longings. Freud referred to this irrepressible inner force as our libido. He contrasted it with the moralizing forces by which we try to control our animal instincts. He thought our moral controls come from our super-ego, and he felt that it usually repressed our real feelings and deep needs too much.

Freud thought that the rational reflections of our minds try to put our animal instincts, our moralizing pressures, and our spiritual quest into their proper places. Freud referred to our rational ability to reflect on these things as our ego, and he was sure this was the mature part of us that could properly appreciate our sexual drives, our moral instincts, and our spirituality, all three, keeping them in proper proportion and relationship.

No facet of a person's life is untouched or unshaped by the powerful dynamo of our libido, our sexual drives. Whether we are sitting in church at worship, in a meeting for business, or at a pleasurable party, we are always aware of the gender of those who are around us. We are conscious at some level of the force of their sensuality, as it impacts us. If we are not aware of that, some wounding has produced an impairment in us that has forced us to repress this awareness inappropriately.

Human spirituality is best defined as our irrepressible hunger and quest for meaning in all aspects of life. Human sexuality is best defined as our irrepressible hunger and quest for union with other persons and the meaning of life found in the wholeness or complete fulfillment that such union brings. At the center of our selves, the life force that drives all of our vitality, or sense of being alive, is one force. It is this life force that we experience and refer to as our spirituality and sexuality. These are not two different forces, nor are they in any way at odds with one another, as they have been made to seem in the polarizing attitudes about sexuality and spirituality popular in human society today, thanks to our excessive and negative moralization of sex.

Western society has tended to moralize sexuality so much that if the subject of morality comes up, everyone immediately assumes one is speaking of something sexual. We have over-moralized sex to the point that no other issues are considered to be moral issues. The corporate executives who engage in felonious behaviors, stealing the money that belongs to the worker's pension funds or the stockholder's portfolios, are considered to have committed a legal breach. The issue of their crass immorality is seldom raised. In our society today, all morality is sexual, and all other issues are excluded from moral claims. On the other hand, all sexuality is considered to be a moral issue. Whenever the subject of human sexuality arises in discussion, immediately everyone concludes that we are dealing with some moral matter. This is a gross distortion. Not all sexual issues are moral matters, and not all moral issues are sexual problems. To misbehave in one's responsibilities in caring for children, managing the family budget, working faithfully on the assembly line, or leading a company is a moral issue. It may, of course, also involve legal issues. To behave wholesomely in sexual play or experimentation is not a moral issue. It is normal, healthy, human and humane behavior.

The central vital force in us, of sexual spirituality, is the essence of our personhood. When it is psycho-somatized, that is, when we experience it in our inner spirits (psyche) and express it through our bodies, we call it sexuality. When it is psycho-etherealized, that is, when we experience it in our inner spirits and express it through our minds and mystical imagination, we call it spirituality. We sense that it is then our reach for God and things of transcendent meaning.

So sexuality and spirituality are the same vital inner force in us. When this force reaches out through our psyches toward God, in our longing for the infinite and transcendent or eternal, we call it spirituality. When that same force reaches out through our physical bodies toward another human, in our longing for the finite and visceral experience of union in that relationship, we call it sexuality. In both cases it is the same force, the same longing for wholeness or completeness, the same desire for communication, communion, and consummation. Moreover, in both cases it is a spiritual quest for the meaningfulness of relationship, driven by the sexual forces of our libido.

If we shear off from one another these two directions of the expression of our life force, or polarize spirituality and sexuality, we pervert both of them. The medieval mystics felt a lot of fear, guilt, and shame about their sensuality and their bodies, their material physicality. Because of their distorted forms of theology, they thought that being a material body with all its sensual drives stood in opposition to spirituality, to the life of our inner selves, and to the ways of God. They viewed their sexuality as the epitome of this problem. As a result, they tried to repress their sexuality for the sake of cultivating their spirituality. The result was that they saw psychotic visions and lived in a distorted—even a spiritually perverted—world of unreality.

Today the opposite seems to be true. Our culture seems in every way pre-occupied with sex and sensuality. Moreover, it has devalued the irrepressible spiritual hunger of the human spirit. This has resulted in an obsessive quest for sexual experimentation that has distorted and perverted sexual play to the point that it no longer leads to union and wholeness. Casual sex, and sex merely for the sake of achieving mechanical sexual relief, shears off our emo-tions from our sexual gymnastics. This kind of "sex for sex's sake" callouses our psyches so that the unity of sexuality and spirituality can no longer be discerned or achieved without therapy.

Sexuality and spirituality are not two different things. They are two names for the same thing: the irrepressible human quest for meaning, fulfillment, union, and completeness as persons in relationship. Is it any wonder that it is mainly in the worlds of sexuality and spirituality we use such expressive words as contact, communication, connection, communion, union, ecstasy, and eternity?

This book is for bright and thoughtful persons of every field or facet of society, for whom the local municipal or university library and the commu-nity bookstores are a familiar place, full of the gratifying tools that enlarge, illumine, entertain, and clarify life. I hope and trust that this book will stimu-late the spirit and surprise the reader with satisfying insights into the one quandary about which he or she always wanted to know and never dared or knew how to ask. In that sense this book is a companion volume to *Sex in the Bible, A New Consideration* and *Understanding Religious Experience, What the Bible Says about Spirituality*, which appeared in 2006 and 2007, respectively.

I am sure that churches, synagogues, mosques, and temples will find in this volume a rich resource for adolescent and adult instruction; and the general citizen will seek it out for its uniquely inspiring treatment of a much-avoided topic for which people everywhere are desperately looking.

ACKNOWLEDGMENTS

I am pleased beyond words to acknowledge Beuna Coburn Carlson for the care and adulation with which she read every word of this volume numerous times, ferreting out all errors, and Frank Shiflett for his technical assistance and for generally ensuring that the book was not eaten by my computer or lost in cyberspace before it was finished and delivered. I thank Suzanne Staszak-Silva for suggesting this volume for our Praeger Series on Psychology, Religion, and Spirituality and for urging me to write it.

CHAPTER 1

SPIRITUALITY AS QUEST FOR MEANINGFUL FULFILLMENT

All of us are designed with a longing for meaning in life. That urge cannot be erased, and we can never run away from it. Moreover, it cannot be repressed for very long. It will always show itself in our reach for relationship. When our daily experience is not meaningful, we feel empty and hungry for something to make life feel full and right. Some people say frequently that they are bored. I usually think that when people feel bored, it means they are not exercising their God-given imagination very well. Life is not boring. It is really enormously exciting. We need only simply to take notice.

However, sometimes it is difficult for a person to notice the exciting qualities of life because he or she is feeling awfully empty inside. Usually what we are really feeling at such moments is confusion about how meaningless life seems to us. We are feeling unclear about how intensely we feel a lack of any purpose in our lives. It is easy for that feeling to slide into sensations of hopelessness and helplessness. Many people are diagnosed as suffering from depression when, in actuality, they are simply feeling deeply sad. They are grieving their lack of purpose, and their meaning has foundered. They are feeling a loss of empowerment and hope. They feel out of touch and empty.

Jenny came for therapy because she said she was "so depressed all the time." However, as she told me her story, it was evident that she was able to express with considerable vigor and excitement her anger about having no boyfriend. She was also quite excited about her fantasy of going for a vacation to Colorado and watching the exotic mountain sunsets. She also demonstrated strong feelings when she spoke of her fears that she would never find a good partner in life. She hated to think that she might be left alone, lonely, and deprived of the children she longed to have.

Jenny was well employed and earned a coveted professional salary. She had a hopeful future for promotion and advancement. She was highly respected in her personal world. However, these good things seemed overshadowed by what she listed as her reasons for being chronically depressed. She was angry about her personal situation of being alone. She feared what she saw as her arid future. She expressed these feelings with appropriate strength. Her excitement about the ideal prospects of vacations and motherhood were all surprisingly intense for a woman who claimed she was depressed. That is, Jenny's affect in all the areas that count emotionally was remarkably resilient. Depressed people have a flat affect or emotional expressiveness. They are unable to show that they are sad, mad, glad, or scared. Jenny overflowed with all four. She was surely not depressed.

Well, then what was her real suffering? I sensed that it was quite important to her and to me to find that out. What was it that she was really feeling? There seemed to be an aura of sadness about her, despite her generally resilient affect. She seemed to have every reason in the world to feel that her life was meaningful. But her story as she told it said her life was fairly meaningless. With a little prompting, she could list all the meaningful things that were really present in her life. She agreed that her job, salary, and lifestyle were in many ways really ideal. However, such a list nonetheless left her feeling at a loss and empty.

I asked her to tell me about her friendships and valued relationships. She said she did not really have any friendships that she would call valued relationships, though she could get as many dates as she liked to have. She also experimented sexually on dates with some of her well-known acquaintances, but she never could feel like she was really connecting in the way she longed to. Too often, sexual play, for all of its fun and sensual gratification, seemed to her like recreation. What she wanted, she thought, was real love, though she was not sure exactly what she meant by that.

As we moved along in the therapy process over a period of six weeks or so, it became increasingly clear to Jenny and to me that she was not depressed but quite sad, and for good reason. Jenny had grown up in a close, warm family of nine children. She remembered her childhood and youth as a time of great joy. Her parents were warm, jovial, sensuous persons who were enormously gentle. She wanted a life like that. To have such a life she needed a companion. But she had never met someone who gave her the same sense of sensuous sensitivity and stable gentleness that she felt was normal and necessary for a good life.

The men her age—she was 28—seemed immature, trivial, and without substance. She could not imagine any of them as a father to a family of children. Nor did any of them seem able to invest deeply in building a generous and genuine relationship with her. She wanted sex, but she wanted to come away from the experience feeling bonded to her lover, not *merely* having satisfied his libidinous urges or her own. Her sadness seemed profoundly appropriate and genuinely warranted. Jenny came to realize that her sadness was the natural sadness of life. It was not a mental illness. It was the way things are when we are longing for spiritual union, and all we can find is sex. She wanted both. She wanted her sexuality and spirituality to be united in an invested relationship with a worthy lover. We worked together on trying to discern how to find that kind of guy.

Our longing for meaning is an expression of deep needs for meaningfulness in our inner selves. That hunger for meaning is what we call our spirituality. It comes up out of our psyches. Another word for psyche is *spirit* or *soul.* That irrepressible inner longing for meaning is hunger for a genuine relationship. We were designed for communion and union with God and with other human beings. In both cases it is a matter of spirituality—a connection that fills life with the meaning we seek. That inner longing is the driving force of our spirituality and our sexuality. It is the longing to find meaning in that genuine connectedness that rewarding relationships can provide. We all long for the meaning that comes from relationships with other persons whom we can really appreciate or love. Similarly, whether we know it or not, we also long for the meaning that comes from the same kind of relationship with God.

Even if we deny God's existence or are not really conscious of a desire for relationship with God, the truth is that we are structurally fashioned with that deep inner longing for God. We are hungry to be in touch with the transcendent eternal world. That is as real a need in us as our longing for emotional and sexual union with a human lover. This is true regardless of whether we are aware of it. So that longing for God is the corollary and analogue of our longing for loving and intimate relationship with another human. Such relationships with a human lover or with God as lover give us a sense of fullness or fulfillment. That need is real quite apart from how we conceive of God or fashion our human friendships.

This book is not a "how-to manual" on more fulfilled living. It is, rather, an attempt to describe the deep meaningfulness that can be found in the spirituality of sex. It is designed to enlighten us about ourselves. It gives names to what we all feel all the time and do not know quite how to describe, discuss, or ask about. It is about savoring the spiritual flavor of sexual play and sexual union without splitting our sexual selves off from our spiritual selves. So this book is for everyone. It will guide the inquiring adolescent who is thinking about sex. It is for the young person who is wondering how to go about sex wisely. It has in mind especially the person who is fearful about the ways sexuality may conflict with spirituality or morality. It is intended to help anyone perplexed as to how he or she ought to feel about experimenting in sexual relationship.

All of us make decisions about such things without knowing much about how to fashion meaningful sexual relationships. In fact, we make *all* the main decisions about life, namely, those about our vocations, educational objectives, life partners, religious and spiritual trajectories, and cultural values, when we are still so young and uninformed that we do not really know what we are doing. That is a great human problem and results in many destructive human tragedies. It produces a lot of damaged and damaging relationships and even alienation from God.

If we make an early decision that rejects our quest for God, we lose the meaning that would normally fill our irrepressible quest. The quest is about meaningful relationship, with lovers and with God as one who loves us. This volume may help make more sense out of all of that. It may be particularly useful in learning how to experience throughout life the rich fullness sex and spirituality can offer. It is a book about living out the sense of completeness that comes from an authentic appreciation of the unity of our human sexuality and spirituality. That is to say, it is a book about the spirituality of sex.

This book will not only inform the quandary of adolescents, but will also enlighten the more mature adult. Are you looking for what is missing in your experiences of sex and your relationship with God? Think about the fact that the emptiness in each sphere may be connected to the other. Approaching these vital human experiences with the understanding that sexuality and spirituality are in unity, and not opposing forces in us, can be an intensely healing experience. It can make sexual life last all life long as an important dimension of our spiritual communion with each other.

In emphasizing the spirituality of sex, I do not mean in any sense that one should observe religious rituals in connection with making love. I am not talking here about religion particularly. I understand that there are people in all religious communities who are so intent upon practicing the presence of God that they make it their practice to pray for God's presence and blessing before they make love. That may have some value for some. Frankly, I like love, sex, spirituality, and relationships with human and divine lovers to be more spontaneous and automatic, as the occasion urges.

However, what I find more questionable about the practice is that it turns spirituality into a religious ritual (prayer) and sex into an objective action in its own right apart from that religious ritual. It makes sex another kind of ritual, so to speak, in addition to spirituality, instead of unifying both as a hunger for and acquisition of meaning-in-relationship before the face of God, in God's world, as persons created by God with hunger for each other and for God. I prefer not to run the risk of making a ritual behavior out of both sex and spirituality and thus actually risk separating them as two sets of differing behaviors.

The ancient Hebrews gave us the mythic story about Adam finding Eve. He noticed how delectable she seemed. He got to know Eve. He got to *know* her sexually and spiritually. They conceived children. The Old Testament believers saw that behavior of Adam and Eve as a fulfillment of God's invitation to multiply and replenish the earth (Gen. 1:28). They understood that our unity spiritually and sexually is a reflection of the fact that we are created in the image and likeness of God. Those ancient Hebrews knew that it meant that we imaged or mirrored the very nature of God in our bodies, minds, and spirits, genitals and all. They did not have the notion that later came into the Bible from the Greeks that there was tension or opposition between our bodies and spirits. They thought that our sexual urges and our souls functioned together in our being God's creatures, and that if we separated them, we would be sick or dead.

It was mainly Paul, in the New Testament, who brought in the erroneous Greek notion that we humans have a war within us between our higher passions of the mind and spirit and our lower passions of the body and our animal instincts. That is a sick notion, even if it is in the Bible, and it has taken us two thousand years to finally understand our bodies and our spirits well enough, psychology and spirituality, to declare without apology that Paul was wrong in the way he put the problem. There is no inherent conflict between our spirituality and our sexuality unless we devalue sex as something God does not admire.

How stupid such a proposition is! Sex was not a human idea. It was a divine idea. That is plain to me every time I make love. It is divine. Sex is like ice cream. There is no bad ice cream. There is only good, better, and best (that last one comes from the Guernsey Creamery in Novi, Michigan). Sex and ice cream are both a divine idea. Sex was God's idea from the outset. God thought it up, designed how it works, and invested us with the irrepressible senses and desires that are inherent to it. Moreover, God tied to it the most godlike of all human actions: the ability to create life. Incredible! Indeed, making love is the one human process in which we are able to completely lose ourselves in the lover. This is just like the way God invests God's self in us and invites us to lose ourselves, as it were, in our mystical celebration of God.

It is clear that those ancient Hebrew believers who wrote the Hebrew Bible, which Christians call the Old Testament (OT), got it right when they understood us humans to be unified persons in all our facets. They called a human person a *nephesh*, a unitary living being. They thought our penises and vaginas were as godly and godlike as our philosophical minds. They did not take the ancient Greek outlook that the New Testament (NT) describes and that has dominated the Western world's outlook ever since. For the last two thousand years we have thought of humans as divided into body, mind, and spirit. Sometimes this has been complicated by dividing spirit into soul and spirit.

It may be true that these four aspects of humanness may be usefully distinguished for the sake of discussing various facets of human nature or behavior.

However, we must always keep in mind that when we make these distinctions, these notions of body, mind, and spirit are just words for concepts in our minds. They are not names for real objects or things that exist inside of this creature called a human person. If you make my body feel hurt or happiness, my mind and spirit will react to you. I respond. I am a whole being, and my whole person will chide you or thank you for making me feel hurt or happiness. A human person, as the OT believers knew, is a unified organism that is of such a nature and function that we can see in it a mirror image, as it were, of the essential nature of God. This means that we function as persons in such a way that our bodies, psyches, and minds are acting together as one thing in everything we do. Our material and spiritual aspects act as one unified agent.

It is of enormous interest that the advances of science in the most recent decades have proven the ancient OT theory to be correct. Psychological and biochemical studies have demonstrated conclusively that the chemistry of our bodies is directly related to the psychological states of our minds and spirits. Indeed, it is now clear that changes in our biochemistry, particularly our hormone levels, directly affect our psychological state of mind and mood. Likewise, our psychological states of tranquility or stress directly change our biochemistry. The hypothalamus in our brains is the central regulator of our hormone systems, and it is a two-way switching mechanism. Long-term chronic stress causes it to switch our hormone chemistry around so as to try to line up with such chronic psychological suffering. Likewise, distortions in our chemistry such as deficient regulation of our serotonin or dopamine level will make us very depressed.

The hypothalamus regulates this by triggering certain chemical reactions in our pituitary glands, next to our brains. They in turn regulate the nature and flow of the chemistry produced by our thyroid glands. Our thyroids are the thermostats that control all the rest of our 40 or 50 hormone glands, such as ovaries, gonads, adrenal glands, and the like. The human organism is a unity of physiology and psyche, of body and spirit. Thus, our quest for a sense of meaningful life cannot be fulfilled except in experiences that hold together our materiality and spirituality. That is why it is so important to explore here the relevance of our interest in the spirituality of sex.

I have a patient who came to see me for therapy after having read my book *Sex in the Bible*. For the sake of the narrative here, I will call her JerryAnn. She presented at my clinic as a moderately tall, attractive, and nicely dressed woman of about 32 years of age. She is one of those lovely women with just enough meat on the bones, so to speak, to be truly erotic, emitting a natural aura of sensuality. She is aware of her innate beauty and carries herself as a person of quality, confidence, and focused purpose.

JerryAnn got right to the point. She said she came to see me because she could not seem to establish a truly satisfying and sustained relationship of meaningful intimacy in her life. She readily unfolded her story of having begun an active sexual life at 19, while in college, and of having had a series of intimate relationships for the 13 years since then. Each relationship lasted for one or two years. Occasionally, between these more sustained relationships, she had experienced a few one-night stands or casual encounters with friends or acquaintances of friends.

JerryAnn said that she had broken off each of her relationships after a year or two because none of them ever seemed to achieve the level of meaningful fulfillment she sought. She said she enjoyed the sexual activity, whether it was making love, having sex, or in the case of the one-night stands, "just fucking." She always felt spontaneous and enormously aroused in sexual play, but never felt like she had really connected with the other person at the point of union and communion.

At age 32, she was tired of trying to fashion relationships that in the end proved less than satisfying. They never proved meaningful in terms of bonded connectedness with the other person. She felt confused as to whether the problem was in her. Perhaps she was unable to really invest herself wholly in a relationship. Perhaps the problem was in the male lovers she had had. They may have been inadequate for a profound relationship. As our work together progressed, this seemed more and more like the right central question. Was it a deficit in her or them? Her childhood history did not suggest any notable deficits in the nurturing quality or stability of her family or community.

In her view her parents had always been tender and cherishing of each other and sensually demonstrable. She had an appropriately tender and deeply cherishing relationship with her father. She had never experienced anything during childhood and adolescence that could be seen as sexual abuse or compromise. Her father and mother were both quiet but highly esteemed figures in the family and community. She and her three brothers, with whom she had close and playful connection, had all modeled the parents' educational and professional achievement.

So we focused on her issues of bonding. At 19 years of age, she was in her second year at a fine college. She remembered feeling free as a bird, achieving well, being full of fun, and feeling intensely sexually aware. The culture of the college was relatively conservative, but the students were normally sexually exploratory. She was made aware of this daily. She decided to take the initiative to explore her own sexuality, and so she began a series of dates with a fellow she had spotted in her chemistry class. The lab situation provided a chance to talk naturally and normally with him. He seemed amenable to a friendship, and soon they were experimenting with a sexual relationship. He was focused on high achievement in his electrical engineering program. He intended to take a commission as an army officer upon graduation. She was busy with her program in pre-law with the intention of finishing law school and working for the United Nations. In fact, that objective she achieved.

The setting and situation of this relationship was workable for a college friendship. It offered her a couple of years of enjoyable sexual play. It was clear from early on that this friendship was not a permanent arrangement for either of them. It was a current entertainment, temporary and self-limiting. Neither of them expected more or invested more than that. When it came time to graduate, they took leave of each other easily and comfortably. They did not keep track of each other afterward.

The 8 sustained relationships and 8 to 10 brief encounters she had experienced since that college friendship had all taken approximately the same pattern. That college relationship had established itself as her original model, so to speak. She had continued in that comfortable and safe model from then on. She had carefully trained herself, from the outset of her sexual experimentation, to shear off her hunger for meaningful relationship from her sexual gymnastics. She had enjoyed the arrangement of mere "friendship and fucking" but had sought no more than that and now found herself empty and jaded in her quest for intimacy. She had cultivated a pattern of dividing her spirituality from her sexuality and was now wondering why sex and relationship were both empty. She was perplexed that they wear out so soon and lose their vital interest and excitement.

Meaning derives from total-person bonding with another person, a lover, human or divine. So when our relationships start at the crotch, they usually do not go anywhere from there, and that ultimately leaves us with empty souls. Unfulfilled psyches and unsatisfying sex result because good sex and real relationship require real presence to the lover and the real presence of the lover to us. Total-person bonding means genuine sharing at the intellectual, psychological, social, and sexual levels.

For a relationship to become whole in that sense, it must start at one of the first three levels, progress through the other two, and finally arrive at the crotch. The reason for this is simple, and everybody knows it. Just take a moment to think about it. The electricity in a connection at the crotch is so intense that it grounds out all other possibilities. We must make sure that the first three are well wired-in before the connection gets to the union at the crotch. Let us face it, folks. Let us be utterly realistic about ourselves. We all know this. It is no secret.

JerryAnn had trained herself to start relationships at the crotch. Her model was that of a temporary, self-limiting friendship built from that point of connection. Thus, the other four levels remained relatively irrelevant, nice but not necessary. So true intimacy could never arise. She had no personal investment in her lover. She did not learn what true intimacy really is. She never discovered the spirituality of sex. She did not understand that it is only there that real meaning can be built in a relationship. So she felt empty, meaningless, confused, and without much of a clue as to what she could do about it. You will understand that it took some time and work to rewire

JerryAnn's psychospirituality and reconnect it with her sexuality. It proved to be rewarding work for her, however, with a really wholesome outcome in her discovery of the genuine spirituality inherent to her authentic sexuality.

People who shear off spirituality—that is, their quest for the meaning of life—from their sexuality will always end up wondering why sex is empty, wears out, and loses its interest. If the spice of life has lost its savory scintillation, how shall we fill it with real zest again? Casual sex, uninvested relationships-of-the-moment, and anonymous encounters, however sensual, may be fun on occasion. But if they become our *model* for sex or relationship, they callous our psyches in such a way as to make it impossible for us to reconnect our orgasms to our psyches and souls. That makes sex merely an animal act, "just fucking." Reconnecting our sex to our souls and rediscovering the spirituality of sex then becomes a difficult return to what we were originally meant to be: reflectors of the divine spirit.

One of the most common relationship tragedies that arises for couples whose model of intimacy has shorn their sexual encounters of any spiritual depth is the disillusion in the relationship that can happen at menopause. When a woman reaches menopause, a number of biochemical changes take place in her body. These directly involve her sexual drive because they have to do with significant shifts in her levels of estrogen and progesterone. Changes in these hormones are not unfamiliar to her because she has usually experienced them in a less intense and temporary form during her premenstrual week. However, when menopause sets in, these changes are more profound, erratic, and permanent. Menopause brings with it a surprisingly sudden and large loss of the need for and interest in sexual gratification, unless the relationship is filled with the spirituality of sex.

If her relationship prior to menopause has been largely "mere friendship and fucking"—that is, if the marriage has not been rooted in a deep sharing of the spirituality of sex—there will be no basis in her model of life for continuing any kind of sexual play and intimacy. Frequently, this is not only a loss of interest in and need for physical intimacy, but also a significant loss at all six levels of connectedness necessary for real enmeshment as a couple. These six levels are connectedness and union at the intellectual, emotional, social, psychological, sexual, and spiritual levels of communion with one's lover or spouse. Too often, menopausal women today, in this age of feminism or womanism, move into a radically new mode of life. Basically it has one primary characteristic: she excludes her husband and schedules her time so as not to encounter him in any important personal way.

Marylou came to me with her husband, Jim. He said he thought they had always had a great relationship. He believed he had been a tender and kind husband who worked well with her in a cooperative marriage. They had raised five achieving and stable children and had built a nice fortune. They had always enjoyed attending church as a family, as well as keeping up a number of pleasant social relationships. Their children had married well, he thought, all within the church community. The children had all done well in their education, had developed good ideals and values, and continued to live a life quite similar to that of their parents, though they were spread widely across the nation.

His sense of their intimate life was that it had been normal, gratifying, and cherishing for both of them. They had met in college, enjoyed each other from the start, and begun their sexual intimacy naturally when they were engaged and had enjoyed married life without any real disagreements about anything. Marylou agreed that his picture of their marriage and family was accurate. She said it had been enjoyable for her. She liked sex, and they were both good at it, but she did not think that they had ever been connected in any way, other than the sexual play. Of course, they had shared pleasantly the mutual care and enjoyment of the kids and life in their community. But she did not think they had much intellectual and psychological common ground.

She had worked for 25 years as a corporate manager with a relatively high salary and felt financially independent. He had done the same as a school superintendent. They were highly esteemed in their community and church, had traveled widely, and generally had a good time of life, but her interests were largely in the direction of history and art and his more in government and statistics.

What brought them in to see me was the fact that she had found a new lease on life since her retirement two years earlier. He intended to retire in two years and expected a lot of shared time with her. He wanted and expected a continuation of their life of intimacy at all levels. However, she had shifted her focus in almost every area of her life. She had taken to New Age thought and was now following the spiritual trajectory of a mysterious India guru whose name Jim could not pronounce, from an ashram he did not understand, in a town in India with a complicated name he could not remember. Instead of continuing to socialize with him and their friends of long standing, with whom they had related in their community, she was preoccupied with a small number of women who seemed to have become groupies of her guru. Moreover, Marylou now spent three or four hundred dollars a month on strange food supplements and dietary aids that Jim was afraid might even poison her.

Marylou had always been a gourmet cook who could prepare any national food more excellently than the natives. Now she had turned radically vegetarian and fed him what he called "grass and tree bark." She no longer had time for church, though she spent at least 15 hours a week with two old men friends at the gym and with a young male Qigong instructor in a special one-on-one class he offered just at the dinner hour each day. Jim had to either eat by himself or wait until late in the evening. Eating late made sleep more difficult for him at his age! Moreover, he could not figure out why the Qigong class was supposed to take one hour, but it always took her two hours to get back. It was just down the road a mile and a quarter.

Even more mysterious for him, he mentioned sort of off-handedly, was the fact that the day the doctor told her she was menopausal, at age 42, she absolutely cut off any sexual play. Marylou did not disagree with any of this report but said she did not have any particular reason, except that now that she was retired, she had time and inclination to develop her many other interests in life. After all, she was spending her own money on it. When asked if she wished to add anything to the story, she told us, to Jim's great surprise, that she intended this summer to vacation with her girlfriends on a river cruise in Europe. She hoped he would not mind.

These two people seemed genuinely kind and open with each other. Indeed, they were quite matter-of-fact and forthright, without loading the conversation with negative emotions. They seemed to be accustomed to relationship and communication that flowed easily. They listened well and readily understood each other. Therefore, it was astonishing to me that Marylou could be proposing and acting out this radical change of agenda and style for their marriage without seeming to be aware that it should be mystifying to Jim and astonishing to me.

It was clear to me that this developing modification of their relationship was not going to provoke any real strife between them. Jim seemed enormously capable of absorbing whatever it was she needed to do, and she seemed to carry it forward with the assumption that it would not disturb her kindness and care for him. However, two things about it were obviously pathological. First, it seemed to me that the degree to which this left Jim deprived of real shared relationship with the wife he cherished was dysfunctional for the relationship. He was deprived of sexual play and the intimacy he felt associated with it. She had moved into another bedroom, perhaps understandably, because she said his snoring kept her awake.

When he returned from work, she seemed always gone on some errand or off with her girlfriends. On Sunday when he wished to go to church with her, she was off with the groupies of her guru. Their friends asked about her, and he had run out of explanations. He had always liked their evening time together, earlier with the kids and now with her, but that seemed to have evaporated right out of their life together. If he suggested a TV movie, she might sit with him a few minutes, but then would say she was tired and wanted to go up and get her bath and go to bed—at 9:30 yet. And she had always been a night owl, as was he.

He was 57 years of age. His sexual desires and needs were apparently normal—that is, as intense as they had been at age 25. His need for intimacy was increasing as he began to realize the limitations of age in other ways, and he found himself more and more interested in those closest to him. His devotion to her and their marriage made the pursuit of other intimate relations unthinkable. What had gone wrong?

The second thing that concerned me greatly was that her change of course indicated a lack in her of connectedness and investment in the relationship. She showed a surprising lack of awareness of and sensitivity to the impact her shift in lifestyle had on Jim. This narcissism seemed uncharacteristic of her pre-menopausal history. I worked with this couple for a long time, carefully and slowly. It was clear to me that if she needed some new pursuits, to explore interesting new aspects of life, aspects that she was now for the first time really free to pursue, such an option was valid for her. If she wished to modify her diet at her age, that seemed understandable. If she were searching for new and more stimulating spiritual modes of insight and expression, who could fault that? I did not wish to invalidate what seemed to her to be an authentic and fulfilling new life after children, career, and retirement. At the same time, I was genuinely concerned about the vacuum she seemed to be creating or had always experienced in her model of intimacy and relationship.

As we worked together to understand what had happened or was happening to the relationship between Jim and Marylou, she became increasingly aware that her pursuit of a rather radically alternative lifestyle was driven by her subconscious desire to decrease the level of intimacy between them. She was eventually able to voice aloud the fact that this had to do not only with her having lost all spontaneous sexual urges as a result of her hormone changes, but also with her having lost all interest in any physical, especially genital, as well as emotional closeness with Jim.

It turned out that although her sexual relationship with him had not really been merely mechanical sex, so to speak, it had been merely a performance to gratify her own libidinous urges. Now those were gone, and so her interest in physical closeness with him had gone as well. So here was a kind and decent woman, for 35 years generally functional in her family, social circles, marital relationship, and religious world. She had performed in such a way that she was sexually satisfied, and her husband believed she was both sexually and spiritually connected with him. However, as soon as her personal sexual needs decreased, there was nothing more in that union with Jim to preserve their connectedness.

If their sexual life together had been one of true intimacy, in the sense of a vital spiritual connection, it would have been the source of their shared meaningfulness in their life together. Then the decline in her libido would not have led to the abandonment of all the other richness of their intimate life and genital play. She had not derived the meaning of her life in relationship from that connection. She had derived it from her connection with her children and her colleagues at work. Sexual intimacy was something alongside of her life that was an acquisitive performance for the purpose of quieting her libidinal urges. It had not really connected her with Jim.

Their union, such as it was sexually, had never become for her a communion of the spirit, so to speak. Had she discovered early in their marriage the spirituality of sex, she would not have become a relationship casualty when her chemistry shifted. Her sexual function and relationship had no spiritual underpinnings; remember our definition of spirituality as the irrepressible human quest for meaning, in this case shared meaning. Without that, menopause and many other life changes will always jeopardize sexual communion because of the lack of spiritual underpinnings for the relationship.

It is of particular interest that in biblical narratives, authentic marriage always involves a special kind of *knowing* between spouses (Gen. 4:1, 25; 19:5, 8; 24:16; 38:26; Ruth 3:14; Mt 1:25). The OT Hebrew words *yada* and *nakar*, as well as the NT Greek word *ginosko*, can have many nuances of meaning, but a prominent one is the meshing of the entire lives of two persons. That is, when these words are used to describe the relationship between lovers or wives and husbands, they always mean a complete union of the two, intellectually, emotionally, spiritually, and sexually.

In Genesis 4 the biblical story tells us that Adam knew his wife, and over time she conceived Cain, Abel, and Seth. In this mythic narrative Adam and Eve are described as having achieved a union that was intimate communion, and out of that connectedness of their whole lives came forth fruitfulness. They seem to have discovered the spirituality in which their sexuality was meaningfully set. Throughout the entire Bible this symbolism of *knowing*, as true and comprehensive union or connectedness, is employed to describe authentic marriage. A meshing of two whole lives within the matrix of the meaning in life, and for all of life, is what both persons find in their relationship. Throughout the Bible this symbolism even becomes a metaphor for our relationship with God. Spirituality is a quest for meaningful fulfillment of our whole persons: body, mind, soul, and spirit. The Bible invites us to *know* God and other lovers that profoundly.

The Spirituality of Sex

The tenderness of passion
Is language of the soul,
Inherent to true humanness
Whatever ages roll.
The touch divine of love's embrace
Can join us as with God
For spirituality in sex
Transcends the earthy sod.

Celestial gift to earth-born man
And woman so mundane,
Lifts body, mind and spirit, to
The urge that will not wane

Until we kiss, caress, and move
In undulating rhyme
To seek that pinnacle of bliss,
Which knows not place or time.

God watches o'er our passion.
Love's language he well knows
And celebrates our humanness;
For there his spirit flows
To each of us for each of us
Through each of us, God's gift.
The spirituality of sex:
Body and soul unrift.

CHAPTER 2

DAILY LIFE AS SEXUAL SPIRITUALITY

Our innermost needs come from what I frequently refer to as the life force within us. This force provides us with our sense of being a living self, a *nephesh*, as the Bible calls us. That life force is probably present in everything that lives, from blades of grass to passionate lovers to God's own self. Both Baruch Spinoza and Friedrich Schleiermacher, very wise and thoughtful believers, seemed to think so. I have friends who believe that the life force energy is present in everything in this world, including inanimate objects such as rocks, mountains, rivers, and glaciers. Just today my friend Maija wrote me to say this.

> Extremely interesting to me as far as understanding the nature of the universe is the idea found in yoga and Qigong literature that energy contains information, benevolent intent. I haven't nailed a source that specifies "consciousness," but it all points to the idea that consciousness is a function of energy.... Perhaps what we're responding to as "God" is a consciousness, a totality of connection that is a function of all energy. That would explain why so many disciplines have cropped up teaching every person to access it, most notably by practicing presence to the current moment, and thereby presence to the energies therein. It echoes the Hindu idea that even stones are conscious. It explains the resonance of crystals and geographic formations, even the ocean or mountains, and their influence on the human psyche. Energy is there in a certain state, and our energy responds to it, in what will hopefully be increasingly understood in a scientifically measurable way.[1]

However that may be, when the longing of our life force is expressed through our psychology and our physical bodies, we call it sexuality. When it is expressed through our psychology and projected through our minds and spirits, we call it spirituality. That is true whether it is reaching for a human lover or for God. Sexuality is sort of earthly and sometimes wonderfully earthy; and our spirituality is more ethereal, whether directed toward spiritual connection with another human person or toward spiritual connection with God. In both cases these trajectories of our life force cannot be split apart if we are to be healthy and whole persons. In both instances it is a reach for genuine relationship with someone we love, God or another human.

As Havelock Ellis told us a century ago, when we use the term *spiritual* or *spirituality*, we should not think merely of mysterious and supernatural qualities. We should think of all those mental and emotional factors that make love a gracious and beautiful art and the source of enormous pleasure, not just for our bodies, erotically, but also for our spirits. Luxuriant sexual expression of our selves to each other generates liberating and harmonizing influences. These give wholesome balance and sanity to our whole organism. Sexual union imparts to our body, mind, and spirit both the psychic and the physical well-being that comes from sex and its spirituality—its spiritual dimension. This benefits each individual lover as well as the couple. It turns a couple into a unified action agent like a new twin person.[2]

This sense of unity between two members of a loving couple is a profound human achievement. "Through harmonious sex relationships a deeper spiritual unity is reached" than is possible in any other way. Ellis declares,

> The complete spiritual contact of two persons who love each other can only be attained through some act of rare intimacy. No act can be quite so intimate as the sexual embrace. In its accomplishment, for all who have reached a reasonably human degree of development, the communion of bodies becomes the communion of souls. The outward and visible sign has been the consummation of an inward and spiritual grace. "I would base all my sex teaching to children and young people on the beauty and sacredness of sex," wrote a distinguished woman [Olive Schreiner]; "sex intercourse is the great sacrament of life. 'He that eateth and drinketh unworthily eateth and drinketh his own damnation' (see I Cor. 11:23–29), but it may be the most beautiful sacrament between two souls . . . 'sacrament' . . . the closest possible union with some great spiritual reality."[3]

It was this profound perception of the potential sexual–spiritual connectedness between a male and a female human that led Ellis to say that our sexual play and sexual union can be compared only with music and prayer, in its depth and life-shaping effect. Ellis quoted his wife as saying, "Every true lover knows this, and the worth of any and every relationship can be judged by its success in reaching, or failing to reach this . . . point."[4]

All the time, everyday, we are normally aware of the gender of the people around us, especially of those for whom we have special longings. Whether we are sitting in the boardroom for a corporate meeting, working on the assembly line tightening bolts in a machine, or teaching a class, we are irrepressibly aware of those around us who are of the same gender as we are and those who are of the opposite gender. Consequently, we automatically have different feelings about the males than we do about the females, and we generate differing kinds of energy toward each. These different feelings and energies may be negative or positive, depending on previous experiences with persons of this gender or that. However, the energy and feelings will be fairly intense and overt in either case.

Our daily lives derive a great deal of meaning from cultivating that awareness and channeling it into meaningful ways of relating to those around us. That is always a spiritual process in that it expresses our automatic desire for meaning through real relationship. It is always sexual spirituality because it is always carried out in a matrix of awareness of the sexual nature of ourselves and of the persons with whom we desire gratifying relationship. Moreover, it is always an expression of our pervasive hunger for meaningful life and union with others to the extent possible.

Most of us do not think of our daily lives as the process or matrix of constant spirituality and sexuality, yet that is probably exactly how we ought to think of daily life. That is probably how we are designed to operate in daily life if we wish to operate at something near our maximum potential. That is, we tend to think of falling in love, falling out of love, being in love, not being in love, and feeling consciously loving toward another person or a number of others as occasional events that arise in special settings. We tend to think of sexual feelings about other persons, even our lovers or spouses, as occasional feelings that come up when the atmosphere and setting suggest the possibility of making love, having sex, or just engaging in sexual gymnastics.

I am suggesting in this chapter, however, that the unitary experience of spirituality and sexuality can be, and is supposed to be, the matrix and tone of our entire daily life. How much richer would our daily life be, on the assembly line, in the store, teaching classes, or in the office, if it were lived out in the conscious awareness of our sexual and spiritual longing for each other, in a conscious awareness of our sexual and spiritual longing for all others. However, how much more special would life be if at least we kept ourselves conscious of this in our relationship with lover or spouse.

We were designed to live in a total-life quest for the meaningful connectedness of mutual shared excitement, joy, playfulness, hope, and sexual fulfillment. It really is possible to live through the various twists and turns of everyday responsibility without losing that overriding sense that our most important and persisting reality is our union and communion with a lover. Jesus was asked regarding a lady who was predeceased by seven husbands, which one would be her husband in heaven. He said, "In heaven there is no marriage, nor giving in marriage." It is quite likely that what Jesus meant was that in heaven we will have as total a relationship with everyone else as we long to have—a kind of holy promiscuity.

Another way of putting it may be to think of our daily life, all day long, as foreplay for our sexual and spiritual union with our lovers. Frequently I hear from people who see me for clinical therapy that their sexual lives lack meaning because they always seems to be in such contrast with the tone of the rest of the day. Both men and women tell me that they find it meaningless to engage in sexual intercourse when they have felt taken for granted the whole day long. This is often the case, whether the sex is really making love or just sexual gymnastics for the sake of relieving libidinal hungers. How can one live out the day with tension, anger, abuse, or simply neglect and then expect to experience meaningful intimacy, spiritually or sexually?

A dear friend recently wrote me about exactly that. She suggested that it is important, for example, to think about the woman who works full time at a high-stress job and then comes home to the main responsibility for the house, the children, and dinner preparation. Her husband also comes home from a high-stress, full-time job. He sits down to read the paper. Perhaps this is the night they have dinner guests coming. She has planned and prepared the dinner, arranged for the children's care, and made sure the guest bathroom is neat and tidy (she does not have a cleaning service) and has somehow found time to do her hair and wear something sexy.

The party is a great success, and the guests finally leave—late and full of praise for a lovely evening. He goes to bed. She cleans up the kitchen, prepares the kids' lunches, lays out the clothes for tomorrow, and throws a load of clothes in the washer. *Then* she goes to bed, tired, wondering what she has forgotten to do to be ready for tomorrow. He feels great about the whole evening and quite frisky, in fact. She avoids his touch because she knows where it will lead, not because she does not love and cherish him but because she is simply exhausted. He turns over, angry that she doesn't "care for sex anymore." She goes to sleep, crying quietly because she knows she has hurt his feelings.

Such insensitivity and neglect on his part during the day sets a tone that does not promote spontaneous intimacy and either sexual or spiritual connection at day's end. The whole day is foreplay if we expect to have joyful sex and meaningful spiritual intimacy. The way we greet each other upon awakening, the tone of our mutuality all day, the overt expressions of appreciation and nurture in those little inadvertent moments that make themselves available as the day unfolds—all set the tone and create the quality of our spiritual connectedness and our sexual fulfillment. Whether we make love in the morning, at noon, or at night, or all three times and more during the day, it is our daily activities and gestures toward each other that form the context of our communion and give evidence of the spirituality of our sexual play.

It really works to consciously realize that the whole day and our entire lifelong experience is the process of foreplay for true intimacy. Then we will be much more considerate of how we behave and how we can avoid preoccupation with all the distractions of work and life. This will make it possible for us to keep first in our minds and hearts the importance of focusing our time and attention upon our lovers. We avoid allowing distractions by others to obstruct our main focus upon our true love. In a true love relationship of spiritual and sexual intimacy, all of life is the setting for opportunities for special times of climax. Every day, all day, is foreplay in a quality relationship that is cultivated with conscious intentionality for making the most of our experience of the spirituality of sex.

Most of us have experienced being madly in love. When we are, we have absolutely no difficulty being spontaneously conscious every moment of every day of an intense sense of mutuality at all levels with our lover. The only reason that level of intense awareness of spiritual and sexual mutuality often slacks off and flattens out is because we do not adequately work at keeping it alive. Of course, there are varying seasons and patterns to being in love, and life's circumstances do affect those. However, there is no reason why those changes in life's circumstances need to affect our sustained sense of mutuality in spiritual and sexual connectedness.

I can hear my wife say, "Try being aware of spirituality and sexuality when you have delivered three kids in three years, and you are up at 2:00 A.M. trying to boil the bottle so you can feed the screaming infant, and all you are thinking of is your snoring husband and the washing machine that is still banging away in the laundry room." Well, we have been there and done that. We had five kids in five years and one more five years later. That was not my decision. It was our decision. It was driven by very pragmatic reasons. I was an army officer, and Uncle Sam was paying for them, so they cost us $11.00 each. When you are working for $3,600 a year on a lieutenant's salary, you have to think like that.

Life has its stresses and strains. I did not like sitting out on a windswept hill in the nether regions of the German mountains waiting for the Russian tanks, going without sleep for days in a row, any more than Mary Jo liked boiling that bottle at 2:00 A.M. with a screaming infant under her other arm. But the real point is that these things do not need to erode the underlying sense and the overriding consciousness of the mutuality with which we loved, shared, made love, worked, and picked our way along the rough road of life together. We found a way to make it meaningful as we went along. Basically, no matter how you cut it, life is a hell of a chronic sore throat. But just because it is a chronic sore throat does not prevent us from taking nourishment from the love of each other, savoring the flavor of life's beauty and meaning as we pass through it, and sustaining the sense that we are in this together. In, under, and through it all, we find our transcendent meaning in the way we cherish each other and are cherished in spite of everything.

A friend of mine, Della Cullins, once gave me a tiny little book, smaller than my shirt pocket, edited by H. Jackson Brown. In the book the author cites Mignon McLaughlin, saying simply, "A successful Marriage requires falling in love many times, always with the same person" (9). On page 41 the same author reminds us that a good marriage is built on commitment and not convenience.[5]

Of course, being in love is a mysterious experience. Many have tried to define it, and few have been able to make much sense of it. In my previous book, *Sex in the Bible*, I tried to sort it out, and I would like to share here some of the insights that were important to me when I wrote that book. What does it mean to love and be in love? How can that become the matrix of our entire daily life? How can we live it so that, whatever else we are doing to meet life's many responsibilities, we are mainly cultivating a persistent sense of mutuality between us as lovers? It is that kind of connectedness, after all, that generates all the meaningfulness in our relationships.

Some think that we are stimulated to the deep, earthy chemistry reactions of being in love by seeing characteristics of our love objects that we remember unconsciously as the way our mothers or fathers looked. We have early memories of seeing them from the crib in our helpless infancy. Now we see similar images in our lovers. Others associate the reaction of being in love with smells, sounds, body shapes, auras of virility or fertility, or cherishing responses that give us the deep sense of peace we seldom experience and perpetually long for. Most researchers and commentators on these experiences think that the triggers are mostly unconscious and that our reasons for reacting to them as we do are unconscious as well.

If we take the biblical book Song of Songs as an expression of the chemistry and electricity of falling in love, we must conclude that the buttons that turn us on are physical, intellectual, emotional, and spiritual (cf. chapter 3). Those buttons are olfactory, gastronomic, religious, and aesthetic. That is, they have to do with how our love objects smell, taste, and respond to us and how they sense and share with us the meaning of things. The things that stimulate us have to do with the powers of thought our lovers evince. We respond to the way in which they appreciate the beauty of things all around us. That includes especially the beautiful way they sensitively cherish our presence, words, desires, values, and longings. Often it seems that when we fall in love, our lovers sense our meanings before we finish expressing them. They complete our sentences before we get to the end. They know what we are feeling before we can say it. Falling in love is delicious and often so intense a longing that it is actually painful.

Now, we all are quite sure we know exactly what is happening when we are falling in love. We are simply falling in love. We see it as a scintillating experience of romance. There is nothing so mysterious about it. The object of our love is a person with so many marvelous characteristics that we could continue the list of them all day and all night long. The delightful qualities of our lovers are infinite in number and inexhaustibly exciting. There is no need to question what it is like, how it comes about, how it works, or where it is leading. It is simply wonderful, and that is all there is to it. Anyone who does not know all that automatically has simply never been in love. That unfortunate person is hopelessly and helplessly ignorant of this whole wonderful world of exotic human reality.

Anastasia Toufexis tried to help us understand this by exploring the underpinnings of the experience in an article in *Time* magazine some years ago. In it she reported on current scientific studies of sex and love.[6] She contended that scientific research, particularly in the fields of biochemistry and anthropology, persuades us that falling in love is a product of central chemical reactions in our bodies. These stimulate the brain with special kinds of secretions, which are dumped into our bloodstreams when we notice special symbolic characteristics of our lovers or spouses, which turn us on. These secretions of chemicals incite reactions in our central nervous system and create emotional responses that are equivalent to getting high on drugs.

Chemists have been able to identify these chemicals and the specific reactions they cause. They are the components of a combination of forces that generate our feelings of being in love. Toufexis wanted to track down the work of those who apply scientific precision to our understanding of this response process and see whether she could reduce the experience of being in love or falling in love to identifiable chemistry. She found that falling in love is a complex biological, physiological, and psychospiritual process. It is driven by a specific human chemistry. Moreover, it became apparent in her investigation that all aspects of this process are crucial to the long course of human evolution.

"What seems on the surface to be irrational, intoxicated behavior is in fact part of nature's master strategy—a vital force that has helped humans survive, thrive and multiply through thousands of years" (49). Being in love, as opposed to simply loving someone in the sense of caring for that person, is grounded solidly on the roots and sources of evolution. The process is mediated through biology and chemistry. When humans began to go about on two feet, their erect stance put the whole person of the other into full view for the first time. Men and women could gaze into each other's eyes, see each other's sexual organs in full display, and make love face to face. The eye color, body form, and libido-stimulating qualities gave each individual person his or her own unique allure.

Toufexis suggests that the electric reaction this evoked between males and females produced new ways of being in love and making love and new ways of turning sexual play into a romantic experience. Now being in love could be fun. Sex could be a mode of enjoyment and entertainment, not just of reproduction. Visual stimuli and the unique attractive qualities of each partner became much more a part of the electricity of the experience of total-person meshing. This romanticizing of the experience of falling in love, of being in love, and of cherishing ways of making love may very well have prompted the move toward more careful selectivity in choosing one's lover. This would have led to the development of longer-term relationships.

Most of us in Western culture have assumed, until recently, that true love automatically lasts long, without any need to work at it. We still commit ourselves to marriage "until death parts us," and we do not mean the death of the relationship, though we probably should. We mean the death of one of the lovers. However, the experiments on the chemistry of love that Toufexis examined suggest that nature intended the intense experience of "being *in* love" to last about four or five years. That is just long enough to get a child successfully and safely through infancy. Today we hope love survives a lifetime, but we are constantly grieved by the high rates of love's failures. Children become a substitute love object, and relationships fail for that or other reasons. The union then ends in divorce or in the even more terrible condition of two people just getting used to each other—inhabiting the same space but manifesting no connection. In such cases the tragedy is a result of the couple's failure to cultivate daily life as sexual spirituality.

It has become more unusual than usual for the intense experience of "being in love" to last for the life of the contract of marriage. A pall of universal sadness reigns in a very large percentage of contractual relationships. Usually both persons entered the union some years before, madly in love and with the real belief that their intensity about each other really would last forever. It turns out that one needs to really work at preserving a loving relationship for a sustained number of years. Moreover, even if one works hard at preserving the experience of being in love, it is seldom the case that one's partner is as aware of that need or as willing to work at it. Moreover, even under the best circumstances, love makes a transition from the passion of compelling intimacy to what may be called the caretaker love of seasoned relationships. To ensure that our love relationships do mature into sustained seasoned cherishing, it is imperative that we cultivate daily life as sexual spirituality.

I know a couple who have raised three children together and are now alone again with an empty nest. I have known them since before they had children and have been fairly close to them ever since. They have never been wealthy. They lived on his rather modest wages until their children went to college. Then she went to work as well to support the college costs. Their children had to work their way through college and depended on financial aid and student loans. During the 40 years that I have known them, they have consistently impressed me with being tenderly in love, always maintaining a very steady, stable tone of pleasure and gentleness with each other.

I asked them how they managed this, and they spoke freely and good-humoredly about it. They told me that they had really enjoyed their times of conversation and of sexual play from the beginning of their relationship. They found it so different from what they saw or heard from other relationships. They realized they had rather accidentally fallen into a relationship of unusual quality. They had made a conscious note of this together and promised each other that they would both make sure this never changed.

As a result of this early promise, they had strategized a pattern of life in which they made special moments for being present with each other for simple pleasurable conversation about anything and everything, just to wash each other with words, so to speak. When the children came along, they saw how easily this could obstruct their times of mutuality, so they had to work harder and with more conscious intentionality to protect such opportunities. It turned out that it was not so much a matter of having lots of time together but of being able to notice constantly the efforts of the other person to make such moments happen. It built a deep base of trust and mutuality. Moreover, these times of conversation were always filled with good humor, often about how complex a matter it was to keep making it happen.

As the children grew, they engaged them in similar times of sharing, but not at the expense of their own times together. They never had money for vacations, but they could go fishing and picnicking and could visit the zoo or fair. They regularly took in the special events at the art museum and often attended the community orchestra performance. Most of the time they took the children, but they always arranged things so that they could experience at least a few minutes of these experiences alone, just the two of them.

Sometimes it was making jokes about the monkeys at the zoo; sometimes it was looking for four-leaf clovers at a picnic while the children waded in the lake. Sometimes it was a conversation about a particular painting by Degas or Van Gogh or about a Henry Moore sculpture. It did not require much effort or need to last long. It was the motive and quality of the moments that counted. Moreover, this all formed the daily context for their very lively experiences of making love. They were joined at the hip, so to speak, and they liked it. They loved it and love it still and are forever in love! They are remarkably unusual, very fortunate, and wise. Their falling in love moved seamlessly into a sustained life of joyful union. From the outset, with conscious intentionality, they wisely cultivated a daily life of sexual spirituality.

There is a chemical reason that love relationships move through the intense phase of compelling passionate intimacy and on to the more mature and sustaining pattern of seasoned love. That chemistry has been isolated and described scientifically. In the studies Toufexis reported, 62 cultures were included. In all of them, divorce rates peaked after the fourth year of marriage. Additional children born between the first and fourth year of marriage, tended to cause the relationships to last longer. Toufexis says that when a couple has a second child within about three years after the first one, the intensity of their marriage tends to last about four more years. But the relationship then tends to get restless or a bit jaded around the seventh year. The reasons for the changes at about the seventh year have to do with the cycle of the chemistry at the root of being in love.

The chemistry of falling in love has to do with the fact that something in the potential lover triggers the electricity of attraction, and our bodies are literally flooded with that very special set of biochemicals alluded to previously. A look, smile, smell, touch, or physical or emotional characteristic—or something infinitely more subtle and unconscious—triggers a brain reaction. That surge of force in the central nervous system releases into the bloodstream large amounts of dopamine, norepinephrine, and phenylethylamine (PEA). These chemicals are very much like amphetamines and have a similar impact when diffused throughout our bodies.

Experiencing a high state of intoxicated excitement, with flushed face and heavy breathing, is natural to the infusion of these chemicals into the bloodstream. That is why such feelings are normal to falling in love. Phenylethylamine is the most important chemical in this intense electric event. "But phenylethylamine highs do not last forever, a fact that lends support to arguments that passionate romantic love is short-lived" (50). If someone takes amphetamines, his or her body builds up a tolerance to them, and one must continue to take larger doses to get the same effect. So it is, also, with PEA. It takes more of it as time goes on, to feel as intensely *in love* as at first. In about four years the body's capacity to produce PEA wears down. "Fizzling chemicals spell the end of delirious passion; for many people that marks the end of the liaison as well" (50). They have not cultivated daily life as sexual spirituality.

However, there are also reasons that many love relationships last longer than the durability of the body's capacity to produce PEA. As the blood level of that chemical in the body declines, the other chemicals mentioned above start to increase. If one still has a lover and works on wholesome congenial relationship, cultivating every day as sexual spirituality, that stimulation increases the production of brain endorphins. These provide an increased sense of peace, tranquility, and security. The death of a partner terminates the production of these chemicals and makes one feel horribly "at a loss." With the cherishing partner alive and present, the body has a virtually infinite capacity to produce these chemicals for *enduring love*. The fizz of the PEA may be gone, but the *more intimate* and *sustaining enmeshment* with one's lover replaces it. Often that is even more pleasurable in quite a different way. Toufexis reports that early love is when you love the way the other person makes you feel, but mature love is when you love the person as he or she really is right now.

The brain also produces oxytocin, which prompts females to nuzzle babies and cuddle with their lovers. It probably enhances orgasms by increasing 300 to 400 percent in the bloodstream as a male or female works up to climax. So falling in love, being in love, passionately desiring to make love, and enduring in love for a lifetime are largely functions of our chemistry. Thank God for such marvelous chemistry! It is precisely that sustaining love-chemistry that is itself sustained when we consciously cultivate daily life as sexual spirituality. That requires a constant overriding and undergirding awareness of the mutuality of meaning we share with our lover or spouse. And that is what enmeshes us with each other, spiritually and sexually.

Of course, it is not just our chemistry that connects us. We connect with each other with our whole persons, if we are mature enough to create truly meaningful relationships and cultivate a culture of daily life that expresses the spirituality of sex. However, the insights Toufexis has assembled explain the intense delights and pains of love relationships. A quarter century ago, Dorothy Tennov, a clinical psychologist, published what became a very popular study of human love experiences. She tried to get at this matter from the psychological rather than the biochemical perspective.[7] She became interested in this question because of her own intense experiences of pleasure and pain in falling in and out of love. Much of her own experience is very helpfully reported in her book.

Tennov distinguishes, as her title suggests, between love and limerence. Her definition of limerence seems exactly like the PEA reaction Toufexis found. She speaks of falling in love and continuing to be in love, in ways that seem like the experience of a flood of dopamine, norepinephrine, and oxytocin through our bloodstream. Limerence is being in love with love. It involves being addicted to the idealized notion of the lover. This is merely conjured up in one's own mind and heart. It is prompted by whatever unconsciously turns us on in our lover. Tennov's definition and elaboration on the meaning of limerence are most helpful!

> To be in a state of limerence is to feel what is usually termed "being in love." It appears that love and sex can coexist without limerence, in fact that any of the three may exist without the others. Human beings are extremely sensitive to each other and easily bruised by rejection or made joyful when given signs of appreciation. When a friendship runs into difficulties, we suffer; when we are able to share our lives with others in the pleasure of what is perceived as mutual understanding and concern, we are strengthened. The person who is not limerent toward you may feel great affection and concern for you, even tenderness, and possibly sexual desire as well. A relationship that includes no limerence may be a far more important one in your life, when all is said and done, than any relationship in which you experienced the strivings of limerent passion. Limerence is not in any way preeminent among types of human attraction or interaction; but when limerence is in full force, it eclipses other relationships. (16)

Tennov's book makes the point that limerence is the source of remarkably delightful experiences for a person. It is all the more delightful if it is equally experienced by both persons, the lover and the beloved. It is, however, an addictive high that is not quite connected to the mundane realities of everyday life and should, therefore, never be mistaken for true and enduring love. That does not make this scintillating matter of falling in love negative or bad or to be avoided. It is a gift like frosting on a cake when one can experience it with a person who reciprocates and is available for and capable of an enduring relationship of true love. The PEA high is to be sought after but not depended on to ground good life-shaping decisions or to produce the enduring love that comes with epinephrine and oxytocin.

"The relationship between limerence and sex remains extremely complicated" (81). Most of the people she interviewed told Tennov that limerent sex produces the greatest pleasure humans can ever know. However, the evidence of the study tended to the conclusion that the very natures of limerence and of sex itself tend to "conspire to undermine the happiness (long term) except under the luckiest and most extraordinary of circumstances" (81). In her preface Tennov says the limerent person thinks the following:

> I want you. I want you forever, now, yesterday, and always. Above all, I want you to want me. No matter where I am or what I am doing, I am not safe from your spell. At any moment, the image of your face smiling at me, of your voice telling me you care, or of your hand in mine, may suddenly fill my consciousness, rudely pushing out all else. The expression "thinking of you" fails to convey either the quality or quantity of this unwilled mental activity. "Obsessed" comes closer but leaves out the aching. . . . This prepossession is an emotional roller-coaster that carries me from the peak of ecstasy to the depths of despair, and back again. I bear the thought of other topics when I must, but prolonged concentration on any other subject is difficult to tolerate. . . . Everything reminds me of you. I try to read, but four times on a single page some word begins the lightning chain of associations that summons my mind away from my work. . . . Often I . . . throw myself upon my bed, and my body lies still while my imagination constructs long and involved and plausible reasons to believe that you love me. . . . After the weekend . . . my brain replayed each moment. Over and over. You said you loved me, at dusk by the waterfall: Ten thousand reverberations of the scene sprinkled my succeeding days with happiness. (vii)

Does any one of us not remember such a scene in our own experience? Oh the delicious transcendence! Oh the painful slide down the slippery slope to reality, that is, to more sustaining modes of love and more durable cherishing. Obviously we are designed to savor and celebrate the delights of the most exotic experiences of love of which we are capable. Then we are invited to cultivate in daily life enduring commitment and caring, cherishing and endearing ourselves to each other. Such a culture of daily life, lived as sexual spirituality, can make life long and good and full of mutuality and meaning. Tennov has helped us understand what it means to love, to be loved, and to love being in love, as a way of living through the practicalities of every day.

I have an uncle and an aunt who were married 72 years before she recently died. They were the two married people who always seemed to be more profoundly in love than any other couple I knew. He became a famous physician, and she was a very attractive nurse. They worked together and shared continuing discussions about medicine; an interest in gardening, art, foreign cultures and languages; a congenial social circle of mostly professional colleagues; and hideaway places in wild natural habitats. They traveled together constantly, worldwide. He was regularly in demand for lectures all over the world because of his specialization on the cutting edge of neurological research. Whenever he traveled to lecture, she accompanied him. It was simply understood that she would, and they delighted in the shared experiences.

She was my favorite aunt and cared for me as a child. I was a small boy of six when I became aware of the fact that they were madly in love. They married when I was about eight, and the sustained intensity of their experience of being in love was obvious to all who knew them. It was about 10 years into their marriage, when I was headed off to college, that I noticed that their relationship had changed. They seemed a bit older, more mature, and less publicly demonstrative, but somehow deeper and even more tender in their cherishing mutuality. I did not understand it then, but it made me feel more secure somehow, at the center more peaceful, a little less anxious and excited about their state as a couple I loved.

Now that I reflect on it, in the light of the insights afforded us by Tennov and Toufexis, I am aware of what that shift amounted to. They had gone through the phase of amphetamine-like (PEA) passion and had settled into the sustaining love of oxytocin. But there was something much more important about what I now remember and what I observed as true of them for the rest of their lives together. The quality of that sustaining love they experienced together for the rest of their years was deep and vast and knowing. They had discovered early how to live their daily lives as the process of savoring the flavor of the spirituality of sex.

They had spontaneously persisted in cultivating the culture of sexual spirituality. It had always been a way of life for them, and everyone could see what a rich flow of deep meaningfulness they experienced, springing from the fountains of both the mundane daily work and the transcendent spiritual hopes they shared every day. Moreover, because they had cultivated this mutuality in their sexual spirituality, the tone of their relationship did not shift when menopause and aging set in for them.

Much has been made of such deep and life-shaping love that embraces all of daily life in its meaning-making mindfulness. This was particularly true of much of the poetry of the Victorian and Romantic periods of the nineteenth century, before the cynicism of the post-World War I twentieth century set in, first in Europe and then, after World War II, also in America. One of the most poignant poetic traditions of that now long-gone era was the celebrated mutuality of Elizabeth and Robert Browning. They both seem to have known what love is and how it can become a life-embracing mode of scintillating daily experience.

In her much loved, singularly celebrated, and infinitely idealized *Sonnets from the Portuguese*, Elizabeth Barrett Browning recounts her own experiences of the love that formed the facets of her relationships and infused with fragrance her whole being and her spirituality. Here, in the chaste metaphors of the Victorian age, we have, wonderfully formed, the poetic expression of the authentic spirituality of sex and love. Let us hear it, taste the flavor of it, and let it wash through us, and let us realize that we too are really capable of life lived in this meaningful mode.

I

If thou must love me, let it be for naught,
Except for love's sake only. Do not say,
"I love her for her smile—her look—her way
Of speaking gently,—for a trick of thought
That falls in well with mine, and truly brought
A sense of pleasant ease on such a day" -
For these things in themselves, Beloved, may
Be changed, or change for thee,—and love, so wrought,
May be unwrought so. Neither love me for
Thine own dear pity's wiping my cheeks dry, -
A creature might forget to weep, who bore
Thy comfort long, and lose thy love thereby!
But love me for love's sake, that evermore
Thou may'st love on, through love's eternity.

II

How do I love thee? Let me count the ways.
I love thee to the depth and breadth and height
My soul can reach, when feeling out of sight
For the ends of Being and ideal Grace.
I love thee to the level of everyday's
Most quiet need, by sun and candlelight.
I love thee freely, as men strive for Right;
I love thee purely, as they turn from Praise,
I love thee with the passion put to use
In my old griefs, and with my childhood's faith.
I love thee with a love I seemed to lose

With my lost saints,—I love thee with the breath,
Smiles, tears, of all my life!—and, if God choose,
I shall but love thee better after death.[8]

Elizabeth Barrett Browning wrote these gentle generous words for her husband, Robert, whom she cherished until her death at 55 years. They were married 16 of those years. We can tell from their poetry that their love never wore out or grew cold, never became prosaic. They never sank into the swamp of merely getting used to each other. They remained warm and active, expressive and rich with the constant cultivation of creative caring. Each year they seemed to learn more about each other and themselves and to like life better every day because of it. It was clearly a matter of focus, intentionality, will, and conscious curiosity about the possibilities of relationship and love. They cultivated the rich spirituality of sex.

Robert Browning was six years younger than Elizabeth when he fell madly in love with her. He knew how to write grand poetry about the limerent or classic chemistry experiences of being truly in love.

She should never have looked at me
If she meant I should not love her. . . .
There are flashes struck from midnights,
There are fire-flames noondays kindle,
Whereby piled-up honors perish,
Whereby swollen ambitions dwindle,
While just this or that poor impulse,
Which for once had play un-stifled,
Seems the sole work of a life time.[9]

They carefully stoked the warm fires of cherishing love for their whole life together. Their spirituality seems always to have led to fulfilling sexuality; and the sex was always explored in the matrix of that world of the spirit that they shared intensely and all the time. Elizabeth preceded Robert in death by 28 years, she in 1861 and he in 1889. Browning wrote with a moral purpose about faithfulness in love, human and divine, and about the overriding importance of the conscious and intentional decisions of the will in crafting meaningful life and love. He often put his words in other characters' mouths, and so he did in thinking of Elizabeth's declining health and impending departure. He has her saying to him what he feels for her. He knows how much it still reflects the fading glimmers in her soul.

My love, this is the bitterest, that thou—
Who art all truth, and who dost love me now
As thine eyes say, as thy voice breaks to say—
Should'st love so truly, and couldst love me still

A whole long life through, had but love its will,
Would death that leads me from thee brook delay.

But now, because the hour through years was fixed,
Because our inmost beings met and mixed,
Because thou once hast loved me—wilt thou dare
Say to thy soul and Who may list beside,
"Therefore she is immortally my bride;
Chance cannot change my love, nor time impair."[10]

There, in that spirituality of love and sex, lies the essence of the wonderful witty wisdom of Shakespeare's observation, "Love goes toward love, as schoolboys from their books; and love from love, toward school with heavy looks."[11] It has ever been so and will ever be. Blessed are those who keep those fires of sex and the spirit burning all life long!

CHAPTER 3

THE SPIRITUALITY OF WOOING AND COURTING

When we notice someone for whom we have a special longing, we automatically express that longing through wooing and courting. These expressions may be very overt or amazingly subtle. This is true whether our longing for relationship with that particular person is a desire for connection intellectually, socially, emotionally, sexually, or spiritually. In all of those types of longing and relationship, the moves we make to woo and court the one for whom we particularly long are expressions of our spirituality—our desire for the kind of relationship that brings us the meaning and fulfillment we seek from that person. Remember that our definition of spirituality is the irrepressible human quest for meaning—deep soul-filling meaning.

It is always wise for us to be consciously aware of who it is for whom we long, what kind of longing it is, what type of relationship we seek from that person, and how we would most like to express that meaning quest. Such awareness will shape the mode and mood of our wooing and courting. If we are wisely aware of that, we have the opportunity and responsibility to make our wooing and courting carefully conscious and intentional. Daily life, well lived, is a process of wooing and courting others as a way to meaningful fulfillment, spiritually, socially, intellectually, and sexually. Neither our relationship with God nor our relationships with humans work very well on a "wham, bam, thank you, ma'am/man!" basis. Both kinds of relationships, with God and humans, require the spiritual process of wooing and courting if they are to become genuine relationships.

There is a sound physiological reason for this courtship, for in the act of wooing and being wooed the psychic excitement gradually generated in

the brains of the two partners acts as a stimulant to arouse into full activity the mechanism which ensures sexual union . . . Such courtship is thus a
fundamental natural fact.[1]

Perhaps the most classic example of the scintillating process of human
wooing and courting is that found in the Bible, namely, the marvelously
spiritual and sexual story in the Song of Songs. In my previous volume, *Sex
in the Bible*, I devoted an entire chapter to the celebration of this surprisingly erotic section of the ancient Hebrew scriptures (OT). It is thought by
many scholars that this book in the Bible may well have been written by
King Solomon, as, perhaps, were the books of Proverbs and Qohelet (Ecclesiastes). If that is so, there are reasons to believe, on the basis of evidence
internal to the book itself, that Solomon's wonderful narrative of wooing
and courting depicts his discovery of the spirituality of sex with the Queen
of Sheba.

The biblical narratives that report the annals of the kings of Israel and
Judah tell us that the Queen of Sheba visited King Solomon because she had
heard of his extraordinary wisdom.[2] It is clear from the narrative that she
was interested in his wisdom because of what this implied about the quality
of his genetic heritage. She came to get pregnant by him so as to create a fit-
ting son to succeed her. In the process, if we can take the Song of Songs as
any indication, they fell madly and permanently in love with each other. The
tryst was successful, and she is reported to have conceived a son and heir.
Haile Salassee, King of Ethiopia, always claimed that he was progeny of this
union between Solomon and the Queen of Sheba (Ethiopia). He was officially
known as the Lion of Judah.

The depiction of imaginative wooing and courting, as well as of the consummation of this lovely process in the spiritual intimacy of sexual play in
the Song of Songs, is worth recounting here. The song opens with the lover
longing for her beloved to kiss her profoundly:

O that you would kiss me
With the kisses of your mouth,
For your love is better than wine.

There follows a shower of erotic metaphors in which vineyard, pasture,
and nard are euphemisms for the lover's pubic hair, vagina, and vaginal lubrication. The beloved's genitals are "a bag of myrrh" that lies between her
breasts and a bundle of "blooming stalks" which is in her "vineyard." The
erotic drama moves with such breathless speed through the cadences of the
poem that it is sometimes difficult to keep track of when the lover is gasping
out expostulations and when the beloved is rising to gratifying response. He
says of her,

Behold, you are beautiful, my love;
Behold, you are beautiful;
Your eyes are doves,
Behold, you are beautiful, my beloved,
Truly lovely.

The passion builds; the intensity increases. The lovers are hardly able to get out full sentences. They cannot avoid irrationally repeating endearing phrases. Their conscious awareness is moving far from their rational brains, deep into their affective psyches. The pitch of passion is increasing. These tender expressions of love are repeated verbatim, and frequently, throughout the song, as though they cannot find enough words. The lover sweetly muses,

I am a rose of Sharon
A lily of the valley.

So her beloved responds,

As a lily among brambles,
So is my love among the maidens.

Then she turns even more erotic in her symbolism:

As an apple tree among the trees of the wood,
So is my beloved among young men.
With great delight I sat in his shadow,
And his fruit was sweet to my taste.
He brought me to banqueting
His banner over me was love!

No metaphor seems quite to suffice for her. She looks for more.

My beloved is like a gazelle
Or a young stag.
Our vineyards are in blossom
My beloved pastures his flock among the lilies
Until the day breathes and the shadows flee,
Turn, my beloved, be like a gazelle,
A young stag upon the mountains.

Once again the lover longs for her beloved, and this time her longing is unrequited. She cannot find him. She seeks him out:

When I found him whom my soul loves
I held him and would not let him go

Until I had brought him into my house
Into the chamber of conception.

The beloved responds with a soliloquy about the exotic erotic beauty
of every square inch of his lover's body. He starts with her hair and eyes,
works downward to her teeth and mouth, celebrates her cheeks and neck,
and nearly gets grounded out or preoccupied with her two fawn-like
breasts. For sometime he forgets to go on. But then he remembers that
there is more of her further down this wonderful litany of love. He reminds
himself,

I will hie me to the mountain of myrrh
And the hill of frankincense.
You are all fair, my love;
There is no flaw in you.

Then the beloved spends a lot of time down at the mound of Venus:

You have ravished my heart,
You have ravished my heart,
How sweet is your love.
Better your love than wine
The fragrance of your oil than spice.
Your lips distill nectar.

He tells her she smells better than a pine forest; her juices are tastier
than milk and honey. The lips of her vulva amaze him. She is like a garden of
choicest fruits, and her scent is a combination of nard and saffron, calamus
and cinnamon, incense and myrrh, aloes and all the most sought-after spices.
From her mound of Venus, her love juices are like a garden fountain, a well of
living water, and a flowing stream from the mountains of Lebanon. His lover
responds by giving him an invitation:

Blow upon my garden,
Let its fragrance be wafted abroad.
Let my beloved come into his garden
And eat its choicest fruits.

He answers,

I come to my garden, my bride.
I gather my myrrh with my spice.
I eat my honeycomb with my honey.
I drink my wine with my milk.
Open to me my love, my dove, my perfect one.

The lover lets us in on her excitement:

I had put off my garment,
How could I put it on!
My beloved put his hand to my latch
And my heart was thrilled within me!

There follows her litany of celebration of every square inch of *his* body, from his ruddy radiant complexion to his black hair; his eyes, cheeks, lips, and arms; his body like ivory work; his legs like alabaster columns; his speech most sweet. In fact, she concludes, seemingly running out of adequate words,

He is altogether desirable.
This is my beloved, my friend.
I am my beloved's, and my beloved is mine.

The final three chapters of the Song of Solomon are a crescendo of competing litanies in which the lover and beloved try to outdo each other in their list of symbols and metaphors for describing every iota of beauty in the entire body of the other. Finally, it all comes to a climax and finale, when the lover cries out for another round of passionate sex, impulsively repeating her persuasive litany.

Make haste, my beloved,
And be like a gazelle
A young stag
Upon the mountain of spices.

Well, anyone who has ever made love or imagined making love with a lovely lover or beloved, would certainly like a sexual romp like that biblical one![3] We clearly have here the Bible's model of the ideal joy and spirituality (meaning quest) of sex. Here we see the ideal for all our wooing and courting. Notice how consistent and insistent is this cherishing pursuit, which continues throughout the days and nights. It has become a way of life for these two.

Someone is going to say immediately, "But I have a day's work to do." Quite true, but that does not need to erase the consistent and insistent mood of cherishing thoughtfulness about the one you love. Work does not need to turn the day away from a wooing and courting process. A tender thought, an occasional phone call, a quick e-mail is enough. Lunch together will do it, instead of some boring corporate repast or brown-bag with the guys. All of these are ways to reach out to each other, as the lovers in the Song of Songs looked longingly for moments to meet. It takes conscious intentionality to keep one's focus on the spirituality of sex, instead of seeing it declining in meaning to mere sexual mechanics or plain "fucking," as my earlier-mentioned patient thought of it. Sexual gymnastics releases the libidinal hunger but leaves both partners empty of meaning. There is no spiritual intimacy in it, no sexual intimacy or real sharing of the experience.

If our wooing and courting withers, and the cherishing stimulation is reduced to just a few moments before intercourse, there is little meaning or spirituality in it and no real lovemaking. When sexual play has been reduced to that, to mere release of the sexual urges, the connection between the two persons is mainly limited to the crotch. In chapter 1 we noted that relationships that are limited to the crotch, or that start at the crotch, usually go nowhere from there. They may last for years, but they do not provide the meaning of intimate relationship or real connectedness. That is the main reason for a lot of the conflict in marriages in our day. People are not investing in sustained wooing and courting because their relationships are basically crotch relationships, genital manipulation. They simply use each other's bodies to masturbate.

Just as is the case when there are financial difficulties, all the little problems of life seem like big ones; so also with sex. When the sex is superficial, all the little problems in the relationship seem like big ones and can easily become the focus of the whole relationship and overwhelm it with loss and despair. When the sex is a good, strong expression of spiritual (meaning quest) enmeshment, because the wooing and courting has been of a high quality, all the big problems in the relationship seem like little ones that can be worked out with mutual commitment to their solutions.

As I indicated in chapter 1, there is one main reason that relationships that start their connection at the crotch tend to be limited to connections at the crotch. It is because the electricity generated by such a connection is so intense that it grounds out all interest and energy for exploring other dimensions of shared intimacy. It obstructs more enriched relationships such as intellectual, psychological, and spiritual union and communion.

Our American culture is suffering from a destructive malaise in that there is little romantic appreciation for wooing, courting, cherishing, and sustained tender relationships. The poetry of the late twentieth and early twenty-first centuries in the Western world tends to be preoccupied with philosophical abstraction, cynical commentary of the most negative tone, literal superficiality, or undignified and crude drivel. I subscribe to eight poetry publications and two notable literary review magazines. The metaphors and images of contemporary poetry are so remote, obscure, and idiosyncratic as to render it no longer inspiring, enjoyable, or even readable, for the most part.

Modern and postmodern poetry seems to be written mainly from souls that are twisted and tortured by the poison of existential pessimism. This was gifted us by the French after their destructively failed revolution of the late eighteenth century. That tragic craziness was not a quest for liberty, as was the American Revolution, but an orgy of killing royalty and the bourgeoisie. The cynical negativism of that French poison spread throughout the West during and following the tragedy of the four failed France-induced wars of the twentieth century, World War I and World War II, Algeria, and Viet Nam. In each of these cases Americans had to pull the French out of the fire, to the perpetual shame of the foolish French. We did so with greater or lesser success throughout the twentieth century. In the process we and the entire Western world were infected by the pervasive spiritual disease of narcissistic cynicism.

Popular music tends to be even worse than the poetry. Not only does much of it fail to rise above the level of complicated noise, but the lyrics are unrelentingly degrading, destructive, cynical, and crude. It testifies to a chaotic and self-defeating world within the souls of its creators. Appealing for altered states of consciousness and celebration of every form of alienation in our culture, how could it contribute in any way to the wholesome cultivation of the irrepressible quest for meaning in the human spirit? It is designed to inspire just the opposite. There is in it no idealism, no imaginative optimism, no construction of models for successful achievement of spiritual fulfillment, and no hope.

Culture has not always been so corrupt and so corrosive. There have been entire ages when poetry was honest, articulate, and wholesome and when popular song, even if often bawdy, was clever, beautiful, humorous, and poetic, a wholesome expression of the resilient hopefulness of the healthy human heart and head. Think, for example, of Ben Jonson's touchingly positive pathos in the wooing and courting expressed so tenderly in his familiar sonnet of the seventeenth century:

> Drink to me only with thine eyes
> And I will pledge with mine.
> Or leave a kiss but in the cup
> And I'll not look for wine.
> The thirst that from the soul doth rise
> Doth ask a drink divine;
> But might I of Jove's nectar sup,
> I would not change for thine.[4]

Or can one ever do so well as the Stratford bard, William Shakespeare? His sonnets are fountains flowing with the juices of spirituality and sexuality. Surely he knew better than us how to savor the flavor of true wooing and courting as a full world of daily life. Have you recently felt toward your beloved anything like this sentiment? "All days are nights to see till I see thee; And nights bright days when dreams do show thee me."[5] Of course you have thought it, or something very like it. So why have you not said it to your lover? Do not wait!

It is quite surprising how deftly Shakespeare binds the spirituality of sex together with the act of intercourse in his description of wooing and courting a lover.

Love comforteth like sunshine after rain,
But Lust's effect is tempest after sun;
Love's gentle spring doth always fresh remain.
Lust's winter comes ere summer half be done.
Love surfeits not, Lust like a glutton dies:
Love is all truth, Lust full of forged lies. (Venus and Adonis)

Moreover, Shakespeare's consummately uncynical tenderness has much to teach us in our cynical time.

If I could write the beauty of your eyes,
And in fresh numbers number all your graces,
The age to come would say, "This poet lies;
Such heavenly touches ne'er touch'd earthly faces." (Sonnet 17)

It is clear that we live in a cynical age in which much money is offered to authors of sensational books designed to torpedo constructive personal, communal, and national values and goals. Americans have worked hard for three centuries to fashion these values. At the same time, honest volumes that contribute to the enhancement of the flavor, taste, idealism, wholesomeness, cherishing love, and pursuit of liberty and security in our culture cannot be kept in print because of the federal tax on book inventories. This is, of course, a violation of the First Amendment of our national constitution, perpetrated by the government itself. However, no one seems willing to raise that issue in the courts. Meanwhile, trash and sensationalist trivia flourish in the book industry, while quality volumes, which could give the Western world an edge on truth, grace, style, and love, disappear before they can be adequately reviewed in the journals.

In such a cultural setting, preserving a mindset that makes life a spiritual journey of wooing and courting takes a sheer act of will on the part of each of us who cares enough to create something of an ideal relationship. This sheer act of will requires the conscious intentionality to fashion each day as a season of carefully tending the vineyard of our intimacy. Thoughtful cherishing leads to the flourishing of the spirituality of sex through consistent and insistent wooing attention and courting surprises. When is the last time you sent your husband a bouquet of flowers at work? What makes you think he should send you some, if you have never even thought of the idea of sending him any? Are you one of those women who *really believes* the erroneous notions that the correct posture for the toilet seat is down? Where did you get that idea?

All kidding aside, conscious intentionality, in thinking up many ways every day to constantly keep the attention of your lover or spouse focused on the fact that you think tenderly of him or her, will pay off richly. It will persuade your lover that you want to hold high the level of his or her joy in life and interest in you. You do not lack the imagination to do that, if you choose to expend the energy and time to think about it. All of life is foreplay, and that is best expressed by the spirituality (meaning quest) of wooing and courting all the time.

Perhaps Shakespeare's most forthright celebration of the gratification brought by true love's lifelong wooing is found in Sonnet 29. He was not insensitive, of course, to the inevitable pain and vicissitudes of life, as we can see here, but he found carefully cultivated love to be more resilient than life's hardships and distractions.

When in disgrace with fortune and men's eyes,
I all alone beweep my outcast state,
And trouble deaf heaven with my bootless cries
And look upon myself, and curse my fate,
Wishing me like to one more rich in hope,
Featur'd like him, like him with friends possess'd,
Desiring this man's art, and that man's scope,
With what I most enjoy contented least;
Yet in these thoughts myself almost despising
Haply I think on thee, and then my state,
Like to the lark at break of day arising
From sullen earth, sings hymns at heaven's gate:
For thy sweet love remember'd such wealth brings
That then I scorn to change my state with kings. (Sonnet 29)

One gets the clear sense from these Shakespearean sentiments that the author had drunk deeply of the springs of life and love and that he had suffered enough in both to be a seasoned pilgrim on this journey of wooing and courting. Obviously, he had found in it all the deep value of the spirituality of sex and love. He was familiar with the human limitations that assail our wills and intentionality when life brings pain. He knew from the inside the intensity and anxiety of being madly in love, with all its electric limerence and chemical addictiveness. He had learned through long years of authentic wooing and courting the enduring love of sustained and sustaining energy invested in the beloved. He tells us as much, quite plainly.

Let me not to the marriage of true minds
Admit impediments. Love is not love
Which alters when it alteration finds,
Or bends with the remover to remove;

O, no! it is an ever-fixed mark,
That looks on tempests and is never shaken.

It is the star to every wandering bark,
Whose worth's unknown, although his height be taken.
Love's not Time's fool, though rosy lips and cheeks
Within his bending sickle's compass come;
Love alters not with his brief hours and weeks,
But bears it out even to the edge of doom.
If this be error and upon me prov'd,
I never writ, nor no man ever lov'd. (Sonnet 116)

William Shakespeare was sure of himself and of the fruits of a lifetime of continuing to woo and court until death comes. He had certainly been there, done that, and undoubtedly he had the T-shirt. We would do well to attend to his grace-filled words.

It is substantially more difficult to discover such inspiring and hopeful sentiments in the poems and ballads of the last four decades. Recently I decided to spend some time reviewing the reviews to which I subscribe, and to read again the poetry and their essays about poetry. I went carefully through the issues of about 10 years for each publication: *The Kenyon Review, The Yale Review, The University of Windsor Review, The Gettysburg Review,* and *Pro Rege,* the latter being the art and philosophy publication of Dordt College in Iowa. There is something to be appreciated about and learned from the essays in these issues, but I find the poetry esoteric and obscure. Even the essays seem remote from life and strangely distant from reality, if not deranged. However, what struck me most about the poetry was the commonality of three themes: ego or self, despair, and meaninglessness.

This struck me as deeply saddening and illumining at the same time. My grief is specific. I am well aware of the fact that the last hundred years have been tragic. I lived almost all of them myself and paid extraordinary attention the whole time. I waded through the middle of the tragedy and took my share of it in economic loss and the wounds of war. However, the last hundred years, taken all in all, have also been the most magnificent years so far in the history of the world, for all humanity. Those who do not think so do not know history or themselves.

They have not remembered the travail of the loss of good sewers and water supplies that resulted from the fall of the Roman Empire. They do not know how dark the pain of humankind was in the West from the Muslim conquest in 650 C.E. to the rise of the university in Europe in the twelfth century, how bleak the hope for most of that time. They do not have the brains to grieve the awful loss of the ancient Library of Alexandria with its million volumes of the superb and sophisticated science and learning of the ancient world. They have not learned of the Black Plague that took away a third of

Europe's population, and the Hundred Years War, which took another third. Nor do they understand how destructive and bestializing were the Christian Crusades, to everyone and everything they touched. Such folks fail to appreciate how primitive the simple conveniences of life were until our time. When my father was born, the implements of agriculture were exactly the same as they were 500 B.C.E., human and animal muscle and simple handheld implements: plows, cultivators, planters, and harvesters.

I understand the tragedy of the last hundred years, but I celebrate the magnificence of its triumphs, despite the tragedy. However, in modern and postmodern poetry, and in artistic essays these days, there is a dour and degrading preoccupation with the tragic—and no mention of the triumphant. It is as though the world of creative minds has been schooled somehow to believe they are entitled to a perfect world, and if somebody does not deliver one to them, they have a right to spend their entire existence bitching and moaning. I guess they deserve the hell they create. The heroic souls of the Victorian and Romantic age deserved the wholesome aesthetic world they were able to hack out of the jungle of their primitive existence as they made it a beautiful world of the mind and the spirit.

However, the worst thing about the mindset of self-pitying narcissistic despair that the artists and poets have created for our culture these days is not the ungrateful obscenity they have made of the art of the word. Actually, we can get by as a society without giving too much attention to literary reviews, though it would be nice to have some really good stuff published by some great and hopeful soul one of these days. The real problem is elsewhere. Their egotistical self-preoccupation and pitiful sense of entitlement, leading to their superficial sense of reality and their false sense of being heroic in their clever bitching and moaning, are a symptom of what has happened to the mindset of the entire culture and society.

I see it in the clinic. The populace is pathological with narcissism, addiction to notions of entitlement, and the certainty that if anyone is uncomfortable for any reason, it is some other person's fault. The uncomfortable and complaining person usually finds no difficulty in identifying who that irresponsible person is. Usually that other person is one's spouse, child, lover, or close associate. Such disposition is inherently self-defeating. Most of all, it absolutely undercuts the life of loving, wooing, courting, and cherishing each other. Yet it is exactly this that is necessary if we are to discover the rich meaning in the spirituality of sex and truly connected intimacy.

How many wives have come to me complaining about the fact that their husbands do not pay enough attention to them? Why should their husbands pay any sustained attention to a perpetually ungrateful and negative wife? How many husbands have come to me narcissistically complaining that their wives do not keep the house adequately and spend too much money, when the wives are working full-time, looking after four elementary-level children, and trying to make ends meet on an inadequate salary, while the husband spends his weekends on his boat in an expensive boat club or hunting and fishing with half-drunk cronies?

How can a wife keep up under those circumstances, when her husband has no clue about his real responsibilities? Our contemporary poetry, popular ballads, and best-selling literature promote these destructive narcissistic attitudes, undermining the possibilities of self-giving, cherishing love. Unfortunately, that loss leads to alienation, emptiness, and the inability to truly connect with another person in any enduring way.

There can be no substitute for the decision to be the kind of person who devotes his or her total self to conscious, intentional wooing and courting of his or her spouse or lover, as a lifetime devotion of constant kindnesses and touching tenderness. Foreplay is all day long. All of life is foreplay for spiritual and sexual union and communion. Nothing will ever make up for its loss. Nothing will ever compete with it for the fullness of life's meaning. Woo and court and never stop. Something of a parody on Coventry Patmore's *The Married Lover* might close this chapter nicely.

Why, having won her, do I woo?
Because her spirit's vestal grace
Provokes me always to pursue
And spirit like, invites embrace. (1.i)

CHAPTER 4

The Reach for Meaningful Connection, Human Lover and Loving God

Obviously, this book is about our natural and irrepressible experiences of reaching out for connection with others. Because we are designed by God for such meaningful connection, relationships with God and with other humans are always fairly urgent. They are also always complicated. The only other person we can be sure really wants a genuine relationship with us is God. The humans with whom we long to have a meaningful relationship may not necessarily feel the same about such a connection as we do. Indeed, that is often the case.

Thus when we find someone for whom we have a strong attraction and who seems to have the same longing for us, intellectually, emotionally, sexually, and spiritually, it feels divine. It feels just as certain and deep as a genuine relationship with God. It really seems as though that relationship somehow makes us whole persons. Our longing leads to a deep sense of love, just as real connection with God gives us the impression that God loves us. It is easy then to feel real love for God.

In human relationships, such wholeness feels like we have found a real lover. A lover is one who desires to share that connection that makes us feel whole. It is wonderfully fulfilling and secure when we find that the lover desires it as strongly as we do. That is true not only of sexual connection. As I have suggested, we can be lovers at a number of levels in our personalities. The ideal fulfillment of our reach for meaningful connection seems to be a relationship with another human in which all six of these levels of intimacy are connected and reasonably complete. Havelock Ellis, in the book previously cited, declared this in his special way by saying that the most gratifying function of the sexual impulse is the "spiritual function of furthering the . . . mental and emotional processes" of our personalities and relationships (79).

Few people have said so much, written so wisely, or been discussed by so many, regarding what it means to develop and experience true relationship, as has Martin Buber. Born in Austria in 1878, he lived until 1965. As a Jewish philosopher, his work focused mainly on the ideals of religious consciousness, interpersonal relations, and community relationships. Buber wrote elegantly, even poetically, about the fact that interpersonal relationship is the most important aspect of human experience and is the connectedness that gives life its meaningfulness. He referred in this notion to the relationship of humans to each other and to God. He believed that our natures reflect God's nature and that the essence of both divine and human nature is our capacity for fulfillment only in relationship.

Unfortunately, much of Buber's work is philosophically abstract and not easily accessible to the general reader. Nor is it always clear just how his concepts of relationship can be given practical application in actual human relationship experience. Nonetheless, his two central points immediately make sense to us when we think about them a bit. He emphasized that genuine relationship is the mutual holistic existence of two beings embraced in a real encounter with each other. Second, he gave new and deeper meaning to his favorite words: meeting, dialogue, encounter, mutuality, and exchange. He was sure that if we were to experience any meaningful fulfillment of our irrepressible hunger for connection with another human being or with God, the first principle was to hold ourselves open to that kind and quality of connectedness.

It was clear to Buber that doing so always entailed significant risks. One could experience the pain of finding no response from the other person, no communion in the relationship, and no union with the other person. One might even experience enticement by another person and then rejection, manipulative rejection. Buber saw this as the inevitable pain of life, but the risks are worth taking and necessary to take if we are to become whole persons, a state we can achieve only in relationship. Taking the necessary risks toward union with another person, divine or human, requires that mysterious and precarious process of reaching out to a desired other person, and yet allowing the other person the freedom to come to us. Buber emphasized that this equation is even, and perhaps especially, at work in our cultivating a relationship with God.

Buber's most famous book was titled, in English translation, *I and Thou*. In this book he developed his ideas about our reach for meaningful connection with human lovers and with God as lover. He asserted that most of our relationships are really only I–It relationships. Even our connection with God and with other persons, whom we feel bound to and whom we cherish, is usually and by nature an I–It and not an I–Thou relationship. That is, when we reach out for communion or communication with another person, it is not the person as that person is to which we relate. It is rather our image or idea of that person to which we are relating. Consequently, we have turned that person into an object manufactured in our own mind, rather than being able to simply be with that other person in himself or herself.

This transaction in which we turn the other person into an object to which we can relate, rather than being able to simply mesh with that person as he or she really is, seems natural and almost inevitable. The only way to avoid objectifying the other person, even our lover, is to consciously endeavor to receive that other person without imposing on him or her our ideas or notions of who the person is *or ought to be for us.* To objectify the other person takes away that person's freedom to be the person that he or she is authentically. A lot of misunderstanding takes place in human relationships because of the fact that the person we objectify in our imagination is really so different from the real person out there whom we are trying to encounter.

Thus, we develop expectations about that person's nature and behavior that are in no sense true to that person at all. When, therefore, that other person functions or relates to us in other ways than we have imagined he or she is supposed to act, as we have envisioned him or her, we become frustrated, angry, disappointed, disillusioned, lonely, and alienated. We tend to do the same thing in our relationship with God. We conjure up in our minds ideas about the kind of spirituality, religion, or divine behavior we think should characterize God. Then when God does not seem to us to behave as we designed God in our own minds, we become disillusioned about God and religion.

I met a university professor who could not wait to tell me that she had experienced an intense spiritual renovation in her life. Her story started, however, in childhood. She grew up in an intensely religious family with a stern father. She never liked him from as early as she could remember, and she was perpetually afraid of him. As she entered puberty and really needed strong male affirmation to develop a good sense of self-esteem, she could not receive any goodness or kindness from him—and he did not know much about showing that to her either, it seems.

Her response to his sternness and to the lack of cherishing affirmation was to move into adolescence with the maximum amount of rebelliousness, alienation, rage, and unconventional behavior that she could conjure up. She acted out at home, in school, and in every social setting and by age 16 absolutely refused to go to church. Her reason for terminating her religious quest was that any God who was as stern and negative about human nature as this God was did not deserve any respect. Of course, the main content of her image of God was simply a crude projection upon God of the nature of her hated father. It was a small leap from there to write God out of her life as a monster. The psychodynamics of that projection are easy to understand,

and most of us in the field of psychology would tend to say that it was an inevitable development in this young girl's life.

Unfortunately, as is so often the case in this sort of odyssey, the young lady engaged in what proved to be radically self-destructive behaviors in order to act out her rage, hostility, rebellion, and alienation. Her relationship with her father never improved, and he eventually died when she was about 32 years of age. That alienation and her continuing unconventional behavior, on into adult life, virtually killed her relationship with the rest of her family as well. She married and divorced repeatedly over a 25-year span of time. Each relationship started at the crotch, went nowhere, and eventually drove her away because of its triviality and emptiness. Two of her marriages proved to be dangerously abusive, resulting in complex and costly legal litigations.

At age 48 she was alone, sick, depressed, postmenopausal, isolated, used up, financially broke, and "going crazy," as she put it. In desperation, one nasty afternoon in the late Michigan fall, she staggered into the sanctuary of an Episcopal Cathedral Church. Dropping wearily and withered into a rear pew, alone in the awesome quiet of this towering space, she laid her head upon the seat in front of her. Slowly she let the atmosphere soak into her bones and awaken some new juices inside her body and soul. Then her eyes fell upon The Book of Common Prayer. It was the old eighteenth-century edition. She slowly picked it up and let if fall open in her lap. Up from the page leaped the words, "Knowest thou not that of thine own self thou cans't do nothing?"

That question turned her inside out. By the time she read further and explored fully what it meant to her, and she felt what it was doing to her, she was thoroughly and permanently changed. Her rage, rebellion, alienation, and fight evaporated. She had constructed her own sick image of God and had spent her life railing against it while her life was literally wasted away and destroyed. Suddenly that sentence sowed a seed of healing in her heart, as it dawned on her that God had always been waiting for her to be able to hear that she had the wrong god, one she had manufactured in the image of her less than caring father. Finally, she was waking to the truth of grace and the relationship that heals.

Today, everywhere in the world, there is a high level of disillusionment about God. Every day, I hear people saying that they no longer have any use for organized religion. That does not mean that they prefer disorganized religion. They mean that they are against, or find no meaning in, institutionalized religion, the church, or biblical forms of spirituality. They say they are spiritual but not religious. However, if you ask them about their spirituality, it usually turns out to be vacuous and undefined. It has no content. They do not know what they mean by spirituality. They are lonely wayfarers without a spiritual map, in the vast and empty world of time and eternity.

The real situation they are up against is actually a fairly simple one. They have had a notion in their mind about what God is supposed to be, if God is going to be of any use to them. Or they have been brought up in a religious setting with a comprehensively formulated theology that describes specifically what God is supposed to be and how God may be counted on to behave. In either case they have objectified God—turned him into an object. They have engaged God in an I–It relationship, rather than in an I–Thou relationship. Well, God is not an object of our imaginative conceptualization. God is a being who seems to behave a lot like a mindful person, if you take the imaginative nature of the evolution of our material world seriously. So God is likely, therefore, to behave as God decides to behave, and that is not likely going to line up very well with our imagined objectification of God—the God-object in our thoughts or expectation.

So, when folks reject institutional religion or carefully formulated theology, what they are throwing out is their own or their tradition's objectified notion of God. That has nothing to do with God, of course. They do not even know God. How can they discard God? They have not allowed God to come to them in an authentic I–Thou relationship, and now they are closed to that idea because they think that rejecting institutionalized religion means getting rid of God. Perhaps the reason many folks today say they are spiritual but not religious lies in the fact that they want to get rid of the God-as-object-of-our-imagination and remain open to an authentic experience with God. To remain open to real relationship with another person, human or divine, in that sense is likely to be rewarded eventually, with the experience of meaningful wholeness. One of the ancient prophets has God saying to us, "If with all you heart you truly seek me, you shall ever surely find me" (Mendelssohn's translation of Jeremiah 29:13: *The Elijah*, fourth section after the Overture, a tenor aria).

Now let us translate that discussion about our potential for relationship with God into the meaning of I–Thou relationships with other human beings to whom we reach out for meaningful connection as lover or friend. The same rubrics apply. Our natural inclination is to think the other person is the person we imagine him or her to be. What else can we do? It is inevitable, unless we remind ourselves with conscious intentionality, in each case, that the other person is a person in his or her own right and is always quite different from what we imagine. If we do not remind ourselves of that, we simply objectify that other person, that is, turn him or her into an object of our own imaginative making.

That always means, moreover, that we turn that other person into someone who we imagine will meet our own deeply felt needs. This does not allow that other person to be simply who that other person really is and behave as that person naturally and authentically functions. Much popular literature derives its intrigue and best-seller quality from the fact that its authors play around with this enigma at the center of all human relationships. We read novels with interest because they allow us to struggle with stories in which people are wrestling with the impasses that develop when conflict arises between who we imagine other people are and who they really are. The intrigue of the novel arises out of the fact that certain behavior is anticipated from a character about whom we have been led to believe one thing, when something really quite different is authentically true about that very character, and so his or her behavior surprises us in the end.

Take, for example, such classic literary illustrations as Jane Austen's *Emma, Pride and Prejudice,* and *Sense and Sensibility;* Charlotte Bronte's *Jane Eyre;* Thomas Hardy's *The Return of the Native, Tess of the d'Urbervilles, Jude the Obscure,* and *Far from the Madding Crowd;* or Arthur Conan Doyle's *The Hound of the Baskervilles.* Is it not remarkable how the author, in each case, leads us to an image of various characters in which we identify this one as the problem person, that one as angelic, this one as the disreputable and an unlikable antagonist, and that one as the promoter of everything good in a character? Then as the story unfolds, how surprised we are that the imagined notions we had fixed upon this or that character prove to be simply caricatures instead of the real person. Indeed, how interesting that as we discover the full story of the real person, the character whom we had already banned as evil proves to be the mature and wholesome one, and the one we had idealized turns out to be the manipulating narcissist or perpetrator of other evil.

I must say, of course, that percentage-wise, fewer of the modern-day novels we find bloating the shelves of our favorite bookstores are as true to life as those classics were. Being hyped by the New York best-seller list, unfortunately, does not indicate the real-life quality of a book. Publishers of popular trivia or topical political propaganda, the kinds that make the best-seller lists, are interested, of course, in what sells and makes a huge profit. That is completely understandable, given the nature of the business. However, that invites novelists to churn out long series of superficial works that are a quick read and that tantalize us with course street language, sensational thriller storylines, virtually no plots or character development, a good deal of scintillating erotica and violence, or political diatribe against high-profile people in our society or government.

Truth and authentic characterization seem to be of little importance to writers and readers these days. That shortchanges us in our need for a good read that, like life, mirrors the enigma that Buber highlighted, indeed, that he thought was the central issue of meaningful human life and relationship. Good novels give us enigmatic characters on whom we can project our shadow sides and the negative or idealized characteristics we usually project on each other, boxing each other into caricatures. We need good literature that will do this for us so that then we can discover how false our images are of each other, how imprisoning they really are, and how important it is to open ourselves to the real person of the other human being. We need such quality literature so that we can learn how to override our first impressions and psychosocial projections upon others and let them freely come to us as they really are.

Fortunately, there are those rare examples of contemporary literature that reach the quality standards of the classics. They do not always get the greatest attention, but they do reasonably well, nonetheless. I suppose each of us can make a short list of those recent publications that strike us as illustrative of the dynamics of real-life relationship, with sufficiently well-developed characters and plots that the ambiguities and blunders of everyday existence are mirrored in them. That is an important catharsis for us as readers, in the sense that it allows us the opportunity to play out therapeutically our own tendency to make objects and caricatures out of others and even of ourselves. We can play out our own troubled or embarrassing stories on the stage of the novel's narrative and the lives of its characters. Sometimes this is possible with books that are not first-rate literature but good psychological studies and written well enough to attract and entertain us. Sometimes they even teach us something about ourselves.

The Harry Potter series was not seen by the critics as great literature. That may have been partly because of jealousy over its enormous success despite the critics. However, it holds a powerful draw for young and old alike. Surely that is because the storyline is so intriguing throughout. Moreover, the fanciful aspects are so compelling and so neatly stacked just alongside of real life that they seem altogether possible and necessary to consider. Most of all, the characters are so robustly expressive of the good and evil in humankind—in ourselves—that they are wholly believable.

The Harry Potter series is a good illustration of the point we have been making in this chapter because some of the characters who seem at first to be worthy actors in the matrix of goodness and wholesomeness fail us in the end; and so many of those who initially impress us as degraded creatures prove heroic and, indeed, salvific by final account. They set in bold relief how important it is to allow persons to be their true selves and work out their authentic destiny as free agents instead of imposing on them our agenda and our need for them to be objects that meet our needs.

The reason we like to read novels is that they give us pictures of our real-life experiences through which we can work out some of life's enigmas and the problems and complexities of reaching out to another for meaningful connection as human lover or friend. We are always at risk of projecting on that other human the person we need him or her to be, rather than accepting and being truly present to the real person he or she is. Buber was greatly concerned that our relationships are truly I–Thou relationships and not I–It relationships. The former make it possible for two people to come together freely in the freedom of each being an authentic self. The latter always boxes the other person into being a caricature that we have fashioned out of unreality for our own narcissistic needs.

When I find a friend whom I can accept without turning him or her into an object fashioned by my imagination, and who can, at the same time, accept me as the person I really am, I know spontaneously that is an experience of love, friendship, and cherishing. I–Thou relationships, rare as they are, when they really happen, set both persons free to be their authentic selves, joyfully and meaningfully. We long to love and be loved. We long to live in the matrix of the spirituality of love and the spirituality of sex. That is, we long for life to be the experience of spiritual meaning and fulfillment, of which sex is a spontaneous and enhancing part. The spirituality of sex embellishes every relationship that it blesses. It makes it whole.

There is another side to this story, of course. Not only do we project an image on other people, designed by our own imaginations, thus turning that other person into the character or caricature that fits our needs. We also do the same thing with ourselves. Each of us is, in reality, many different selves. It is possible to create a taxonomy of the various selves that we are or see ourselves to be. By taxonomy I mean here a stack of categories that describe the ways we see ourselves, are seen by others, or really are inherently. For example, somewhere in that stack is the person that I really am, even if it is not consciously clear to me who that is. Somewhere above or below that real self is the self I think I really am. For healthy persons that perceived self is usually somewhat more positive, or higher in the stack, than the real self. If I am depressed, however, I will see myself as less than I really am.

Higher in the stack is the person I would like to be, above that the self I idealize, and perhaps for rather notable people, somewhere above that the person others idealize them to be. Somewhere below the person I really am lies my shameful or guilty self, when I feel I have done wrong or failed. Lower yet is my demeaned self and further down my damaged self, if I have gotten myself into a disposition of feeling like I am falling far short of the idealized self that I envision. Indeed, if I over-idealize myself as someone much more than I really am, and then from that idealized position, I look down the stack at my real self, it looks to me like that real self is much further down the stack than it really is. It is like looking through a telescope backward. In such a case I see my real self as a demeaned or damaged self and begin to denigrate myself, because I view myself as way down at the bottom of all possibilities.

We do exactly that with others. We meet a person for whom we feel intense longing. We magically idealize that person far beyond his or her real qualities. We expect that person to enhance our lives enormously. Then we get acquainted with that real person, and he or she falls so much short of our idealization that we demean him or her as being a serious disappointment. Sometimes it works in reverse. We think relatively negatively of a person and try to have nothing to do with him or her, but life throws us into interaction with that person, and we discover that he or she is remarkably more ideal than we expected. That may lead us to a deep appreciation or even to an over-idealization of him or her. In our reach for meaningful connection with human or divine lovers, it is quite important that we, with conscious intentionality, open ourselves to the other person and allow him or her to come to us as the authentic person that he or she is. At the same time it is important that we have some reasonably good idea of our own real selves and offer those authentic selves honestly and freely to the relationship.

There are some structural problems inherent in the reach of men and women for each other. There are gender and biochemical differences between males and females that become evident when we are drawn into the search for meaningful connection. Because these are not generally understood in society, they cause much more jeopardy to the spirituality of sex than we expect or imagine. Take, for example, the unconscious or intuitive desires and expectations that men and women have regarding the outcome of wooing and courting. It seems generally clear that in our reach for each other, men and women behave quite similarly. We express various levels of intensity in our desire to love and be loved, to cherish and be cherished, to touch, fondle, kiss, give gifts of love and kindness, and behave so as to delight the other person. We desire to have those exact kinds of experiences given to us, in turn, by the one we reach out to.

Thus, as a couple develops their relationship and cultivates their experiences of intimacy, intellectually, emotionally, spiritually, and sexually, it appears that each has the same longing as the other. Each seems to experience the intensity of love just like and in the same way as the other. Both seem to have a very similar desire to find their "other half," so to speak, in their partner, thus experiencing their longed-for wholeness. However, when that love relationship produces children, a discernable shift of forces and dynamics is usually seen in the relationship between the spouses. The man still longs to find his completeness in his wife, but his wife now finds her completeness in the children.

How often, for example, is it not the case that this shift in her outlook from wife to mother brings with it an intense shift in the relationship of the marriage? She has radically changed her expectations, while her husband's expectations remain the same as before. He still loves her in the way he always did and wants to find his wholeness in the marriage. She loves him, but not in the way she seemed to before. She wants to find her wholeness in her children, unconsciously assigning her husband, in the process, the caretaker role. Formerly, his role was the same as his expectation, namely, to celebrate the joy of the coupled relationship. Now his role is that of provider of intimacy when his wife desires it, of financial resources if she cannot do so by inheritance or employment, and of general caretaker of the security and comfort of the family.

In such a case, what was his central experience of union with his wife is now frosting on the cake, if it is available at all; the cake itself is the nurture and support of the family in all the ways families need care. This may not be an *unfortunate* shift in dynamics in the relationship, but it is a *dramatic* and *radical* shift. Moreover, it is almost inevitable. In the worst-case scenario, when the wife is particularly narcissistic, the husband will get the clear message that he is in the way, unnecessary, unwanted, and a pest, except for his ability for providing the paycheck. She will make it clear in subtle or overt ways that he is peripheral to her life and perhaps to the family's life, and he should stop being a bother.

If this happens, it is a tragic state of affairs. It can develop only when the relationship was not built with adequate intimacy at all six levels in the first place, or when the union was never authentic because of narcissistic and acquisitive pathology in her personality. It is clear in this tragic case that she never loved him as he loved her. She may not have been aware of that fact. She may have thought and felt that her longing for union with him was the same as his longing for her. He undoubtedly would have seen the relationship in that same way.

However, now the truth comes out. Her preoccupation with finding her wholeness in the children at the expense of her relationship with her husband makes it clear that from the outset her love for him was merely the unconscious ulterior motivation to get her womb filled. Now that her womb hunger is satisfied, "he has made her a real woman," as they used to say; she has no further emotional or spiritual use for him. She will try to keep him around for her material benefit only.

Comparable pathologies of narcissism and ulterior motives may exist in his personality as well, of course, but they usually produce different obstructions to real union, and at a much earlier moment in the relationship. The pattern that often develops in men when they are starting their careers, a thing that typically takes place at just the time when the children start to arrive, can have similar consequences for the relationship. Men often escape into supporting the family, laying the foundations for building the estate, and adding to their capacity for advancement in their careers by taking the time to get additional training or education. They often use this as an excuse for depriving their wives and children of real relationship. This can result in the attitude that their wives should handle things at home and not get in the way. This devalues everyone in the family.

In their difficult but important book about Jungian psychoanalytic perspectives on these kinds of relationship issues, Halligan and Shea offer us a chapter by Robert L. Moore.[1] He makes a helpful point that illumines our discussion at just this juncture. He contends that the important contribution of Carl Jung, the famous Swiss psychoanalyst, lay in the powerful intuitions he shared with us about the deep nature of our human selves. Jung was sure that one of the four elements of which we are psychospiritually formed, at the center of our selves, is that of lover. We inherently need to love and be loved.

The question is whether we attach our hunger *to* love and *for* love to our jobs, our kids, our careers, a large estate, a promotion, or to our spouse and lover.

Moore interprets Jung as claiming that any human who expects to achieve a gratifying degree of quality in wholeness must be very much aware of the importance of spiritual wholeness, namely, a fully satisfying experience of truly meaningful life. Moreover, any human who seeks a spirituality of wholeness, and therefore a spirituality of sex, must not only mature into a fully orbed person in his or her self. He or she must also facilitate, encourage, and make room for a spirituality of wholeness and sexuality that honors and empowers the full range of expressions of the self in the other person to whom he or she is reaching out for meaningful connection. Mature persons seeking authentic union in their relationships, with all or most of the six levels of intimacy fully alive and well, will always need to encourage and empower their mates to be truly and authentically their full selves. Thus mature persons provide the freedom of operation for their spouses, friends, or lovers to become mature, as well, and to fashion a free and authentic individuality.

A husband who is patriarchal and bossy in his relationship with his wife has shifted that union from a husband–wife model to a father–daughter model, with a bad father-style at that. He has betrayed his wife by imposing a set of expectations on the relationship that prevents true union at the six levels of intimacy. In exactly the same way, a wife who shifts from the role of wife to the role of mother, once her womb hunger is filled, is putting her husband on the shelf as peripheral to the meaning of her life. She has betrayed him. Moreover, she has betrayed herself and her children as well. It is astonishing how frequently this happens in American families. It is a national tragedy.

M. Joycelyn Elders, in her foreword to Marie M. Fortune's book *Love Does No Harm*, makes this observation on the matter.

> While intimate relationships have always been problematic, it seems in recent years we are witnessing a great deal of breakdown in our society . . . In so many instances, relationships just do not seem to be what they should. Too many people have been left in a state of pain, shame, denial, helplessness, and hopelessness. . . . we must realize that now, more than ever, it is crucial . . . that we be open to expanding our understanding . . . so we can . . . reach the goal of finding healthy solutions.[2]

James B. Nelson says of Fortune's book that it is a realistic book that nourishes our capacity for cultivating the ability to choose how to act in keeping with our values, with our eyes wide open to the effect we have on our spouses, friends, or lovers. He emphasizes that this is a book about love but not one that is sentimental about it. Instead it is tough-minded and hard hitting and hopeful. It is hopeful because it emphasizes the fact that if we are to be mature persons, we must cultivate the practice of doing the most good and the least harm in our relationships.

As noted earlier, mature persons seeking authentic union in their relation-ships need to encourage and empower their mates to be truly and authenti-cally their full selves, providing the freedom of operation for their spouses, friends, or lovers to be mature as well. Nelson makes this observation regard-ing Fortune's work:

> She knows that as human beings we are so radically relational that our loves of God, self, and . . . partner . . . are finally inseparable. Self-love is necessary grounding for love of the partner, and when we truly love an-other human being we are at the same time loving God. . . . Marie Fortune knows . . . how capable we are of doing great harm in our sexual relation-ships. Even more fundamentally, she knows that our very nature makes us desire intimacy. We are created hungry for connection. We are fated with the will to communion. Our fundamental human craving is to belong, and our root anxiety is that of not belonging. God is love, and we are destined to be lovers. Correspondingly, our sin is estrangement from love, life in which fulfilling connection is broken, life in which our choices express our lives in distorted ways. . . . However, even when our loves are destructively distorted they strangely reveal our intended destiny. Our most warped and harmful loves are still desperate attempts to find connection. I believe that such an understanding of human nature paradoxically gives solid hope for our human transformation.[3]

Fortune suggests a set of guidelines that make mature, healthy, and ful-filled relationships possible and even likely. First, she suggests that the abil-ity to relate to another with real openness, which frees both oneself and the lover to be authentic selves, is greatly helped when the intimate partner we choose is a person who has personal strengths similar to our own. Equal personal strengths means spiritual, intellectual, psychological, emotional, sexual, and social power or abilities that function approximately as well in each of us. Second, a mature relationship requires that both partners are ap-proximately equal in enthusiasm for the relationship and so can be equally attentive to it and caring about it.

Third, a truly open and free relationship of mature style and quality, as has been described, is one in which both persons are strongly committed to kindness and to carefully protecting their partner from any kind of harm. Cooperation and development time is required to get to the point at which the relationship reflects this quality of caring. Fourth, mature relationship involves joyful delight in tending to the needs of our spouses, friends, or lov-ers as much as to our own, with the confident sense that the same quality of tending and tenderness will be reciprocated. Finally, mature relationships cultivate the sense of freedom in the other, freedom to come to the relation-ship freely and openly as an authentic self. We cultivate this sense of freedom by making sure that our promises are kept, that the expectations we create in our lovers are fulfilled, that honesty and fidelity reign in our connected-ness, and that we can be counted on to adapt constructively and lovingly to inadvertent and unexpected changes that inevitably arise in life.

We spontaneously reach for meaningful connections with others every day of our lives. That motive and the longing that drives that reach are inherent to our natures. We are persons who wish, in our deepest being, to be lovers. We are designed like God is, to love and be loved in relationship to human lovers and our divine lover. Such a gift will be most fulfilling when it is the driver for doing good and the motive to do no harm. Doing good in love will best be realized when it is the mature expression of a free and open person inviting intimacy with another free and authentic beloved.

I reach for you
As I imagine you.
I know what I need you to be;
But I want you to be you
And I want to still want you
When I discover the real you;
But I do not know what I will do
With the real you
When I discover you
Are not the you that I perceived
I needed you loving me
To be, as I saw myself
When I found myself drawn to you.
Please help me to embrace the real you.
Please be yourself
And come to me as you,
Open, free. Take me as I am
So I am free to be me
Not just as I see myself
But as I discover myself
In loving the real authentic you.

CHAPTER 5

THE PSYCHOSPIRITUALITY OF COMMUNION, UNION, ECSTASY, AND ETERNITY

It is interesting that in our quest for fulfilling relationships, there is a unique set of words that speak to that special quest. These words are special in describing both our spiritual and our sexual experiences. The words are *contact, connection, communication, communion, union, ecstasy,* and *eternity.* That set of words fits no other setting or aspect of human experience in the precisely expressive way that it describes human sexuality and spirituality. Moreover, that verbal equation describes a crescendo of emotional intensity that reminds one of the progress from foreplay to sexual orgasm, or from religious reflection to spiritual vision, trance, and enlightenment. This verbal crescendo and its implied or symbolized psychospiritual climax is an aesthetic model of how our innermost selves reach for and achieve fullness, meaningful fulfillment—a whole life.

Falling in love, being in love, living with a loved one, and making love are all processes on a continuum of growth. They start somewhere at some moment, they progress through a process of steadily increasing intensity, and they reach a point of meaningful fulfillment. For that process to develop, not only must both persons in the love relationship be open to the authentic self of the other, as described previously, but each person must also allow the lover in. That is, both persons must be players. The contact cannot become a connection, nor can the connection grow into communion, if one person is a player, and the other is merely a spectator. The spirituality of sex is grown as a result of the active cultivation of it by both partners. Relationship that can become both genuine and open requires that we be independent individuals who give ourselves to the enmeshment of a union. For that to happen we must be allowed into the lover's inner self.

> Love prefers the good of another to my own, but it does not even compare the two. It has only one good: that of the beloved, which is, at the same time, my own. Love shares the good with another not by dividing it with him [or her] but by identifying itself with him [or her] so that his [or her] own good becomes my own.[1]

I am interested in and mystified by the fact that I frequently see young couples today walking on the street, sitting in the park, or shopping together while both have on earphones, listening presumably to their preferred music. They may well be listening to the same music, or maybe not. What mystifies me is the extent to which, though they are apparently a couple, they are living those moments in highly individualized worlds. One thing is clear: in whatever way their relationship is coupled, they are maintaining their individuality. The interesting question is whether they have fashioned their coupled world without each letting the other in. They do not seem to be sharing the same psychological, social, or intellectual space, theme, focus, or fun. Even if they are listening to the same music, their reception of it is not a shared experience. Each lives in his or her own world. That does not cultivate union.

One sees similar behavior today on the part of many people who are not lovers or couples but members of families. Yesterday I observed a family of two parents and five pubescent and adolescent children driving down a street near my home. I happened to observe them for some considerable time because it turned out that they were heading for the same restaurant that I intended to visit. They entered the establishment just after me and sat in a booth near my table. During the car ride and the entire family meal, each of the children wore earphones and seemed to be lost in some ethereal world of cyberspace. Needless to say, no family conversation took place during the entire time I observed this group of "loved ones." Perhaps a clue to the reason for this individualistic pattern of isolation lies in the fact that during the entire family meal, neither parent spoke to the other, though they were not wearing earphones. They did not seem tense or upset with each other. They simply had nothing to say to each other.

Genuine individuality is, of course, necessary for authentic relationship to occur. Two persons who make contact and connect, growing then to communion and union, must retain their individual personhood. If not, there are no persons to have a relationship. In such a case, the coupling becomes a mere glancing off each other, so to speak, like two objects bumping into each other with no union; or oppositely, a contact that is merely a dependency, like a ball of sticky glue, in which one or both personalities is lost in the glob that substitutes for relationship. The psychospirituality (shared meaning) of communion, union, ecstasy, and eternity is a lively experience of neither independence nor dependence, but the vibrant work and play of

interdependence. That takes two individuals who are free to choose a union
in which each gives his or her self to the other and allows the other into his
or her own self as well.

I have attended many weddings. They are very interesting ceremonies,
worth watching carefully for all the symbolic behavior that one can witness.
First of all, I get the impression that in America these days, weddings are
really community fertility rites. Nowhere else in American society do women
dress so sensually and with such overt sexual display as at American weddings where they are guests. They are surprisingly creative, artistically aesthetic, and delightful in the way they dress and show off their God-given
endowments. Even if I were not invited to weddings, I would try to go to as
many as I could just to see the inordinate female self-expression. I suppose
that the unconscious motivation for such erotic display relates to everyone's
wish that the newly married couple will enjoy all the rich fertility and fullness of the sexual component of true psychospiritual communion, union, and
ecstasy. Of course, we all wish that for ourselves and for everyone else. It is
simply an expression of our irrepressible longing for complete fulfillment in
love and intimacy.

However, one of the most meaningful moments in a wedding is the lighting of the unity candle by the newly married couple. The lighted unity
candle symbolizes their genuine union. However, the thing to watch for
after they light that unity candle is what they do with the candle tapers they
used to light that unity candle. Those two candles stand on the altar and are
lighted before the ceremony starts. They symbolize the individuality of the
two persons who come together to be married. The two candles symbolize the fact that they come from their own individual worlds to join each
other at the altar, there to create a new world of coupled union. So what do
they do with the two individual candles after the unity candle is lit? Some
couples extinguish the two individual candles. Others allow them to remain
lit, so that the altar holds the two individual candles and the unity candle
between them.

Does all that mean anything? Well, of course, it depends on how thoughtful a person is, how symbolically aware one is, and what meanings one brings
to that moment and those symbols. However, some couples extinguish the
individual candles with the specific intent of symbolizing the fact that in
marriage they give up their individuality and become a union in which individuality does not function. Other couples keep the two individual candles
lit, symbolizing that here we have two whole, open, and free persons forming a communion and union in which each will operate in such a way as to
pour himself or herself out for the cherishing of the other, and each will
allow the other in without reservation. Their union is not a glob of sticky
glue, however, which would represent dependency. Their union represents
a relationship of two persons joining in devoted interdependence. Their

individual candles stay lighted while the candle of their unity, nonetheless, burns brightly.

It is interesting that when the unity candle first came to be used generally in American weddings, sometime in the late 1950s, the meaning accorded this symbolism was that of the individuals losing their individuality in the union. The two individual candles were always extinguished, leaving only the unity candle burning. By the late 1970s, a remarkable shift had taken place, undoubtedly a good one, to leaving the individual candles lit, after the lighting of the unity candle. This represented a shift in society and in American culture toward a stronger emphasis on the importance of each participant in a union of love retaining the authentic selfhood that, then, can be honestly given to the other in the relationship. This implied that each lover was a player, and neither was merely a spectator.

Thomas Merton, a Trappist monk, had revealing words to say about this: "The gift of love is the gift of the power and the capacity to love, and, therefore, to give love with full effect is also to receive it. So, love can only be kept by being given away, and it can only be given perfectly when it is also received."[2] With that expression in mind, we can see the relevance he gave to the following poetic words.

Love is our true destiny.
We do not find the meaning of life
By ourselves alone.
We find it with another.

We do not discover the secret of our lives
Merely by study and calculation
In our own isolated meditations.
The meaning of our life is a secret
That has to be revealed to us in love,
By the one we love.

If this love is unreal,
The secret will not be found,
The meaning will never reveal itself,
The message will never be decoded.
At best, we will receive a scrambled and partial message,
One that will deceive and confuse us.
We will never be fully real
Until we let ourselves fall in love,
With another human person,
Or with God.[3]

Clearly, Merton would not understand young people who think they have a relationship when they are lost in the isolation of cyberspace, with the real world of relationship muffled out by earphones and replaced by some virtual world of unreality. He calls us to reach for meaningful connection with a lover, human or divine. He implies that taking off the earphones long enough for sexual gymnastics, only to return to cyberspace, does not constitute relationship. It is not real coupling and cannot become the road to connection, communion, and union, to say nothing about any kind of deeply meaningful ecstasy. Merton was a monk, but he had much to say about the importance of sexual, as well as spiritual, union. He saw shared spirituality always leading to and giving deep meaning and quality to sexuality. He understood clearly the precious reality of the spirituality of sex.

One of the more interesting and humorous aspects of human life is the fact that all of us believe, when we reach adolescence, that *we* have invented sex and that former generations just do not know what we know about it. As a result, few of us are able to inquire or hear from previous generations what might be very good advice about building meaningful intimate relationships. That is probably one of the main reasons that responsible and mature folks do not try harder to share these important insights with adolescents. Adolescents cannot listen to us on this point. They know better.

In any case, the net result in almost every culture, human community, and family is the failure of each generation to pass down to their children the crucial insights we have been discussing about the spirituality of sex. What adolescent is going to be able to hear any wise counsel about the development of this wonderful potential experience of contact, connection, communion, union, ecstasy, and eternity? Perhaps this book will be a useful tool for parents who would like their young people to really understand this.

Most of us reach midlife before we are able to perceive these insights about our own natures, in life and love, well enough to ask the questions and be open to the answers that this book discusses. Moreover, we are all born with a fairly strong hesitation about allowing ourselves to be truly known by another person, so it is difficult to speak with others, perhaps particularly our children, and they with us, about those intimate aspects of ourselves that are so mysterious and unknown to ourselves.

> There is a tremendous risk in letting ourselves be known. . . . So out of fear we try always to guard our innermost selves from exposure. But when we do that, we cut ourselves off from the very solution to our alienation. The walls that protect us from rejection also protect us from the joy of being accepted, of knowing that when we open up the areas of our lives where we are hurting and vulnerable, we can be cared for [loved and cherished]. When couples harbor secrets from each other, they prevent their bond from becoming complete. . . . We submit ourselves to the dangers of intimacy [nonetheless] because we cannot help ourselves. Try as we might,

we cannot escape our God-given need to belong to someone. . . . We need to have another person inside.[4]

Whether that becomes possible for us depends on how we define our own expectations. Those definitions are usually unconscious in us, and we do not often revisit them to see what our real meanings regarding relationship actually are. We are often so busy living that we do not think to ask ourselves about the meaning of our living. People tend unconsciously to define their expectations of relationships in fractured terms. Love or relationship is often defined as loyalty, affection, emotional understanding, sex, performance of the honey-do list, or romance of some undefined sort.

However, real love is the whole person of one individual connecting with the whole person of another human being. All six levels are important: intellectual, psychological, emotional, social, sexual, and spiritual. At the center it is a connection of two hearts. You cannot divide that up into pieces of this or that sort. Moreover, the wonderful thing about this is that, in the end, the whole psychospiritual experience of the communion, union, and ecstasy of love is more than the sum total of all the parts of it put together.

> Love implies the coming together of two people in such a way that they open themselves fully and share themselves with each other. They talk and listen, eager to be in touch with each other at the deepest level. In the process, all that they are—background, culture, preferences, and prejudices—is offered up to the other and becomes vulnerable to change. They connect with each other, respond to each other, affect each other— and they are never the same persons they were before they let each other into their lives. Love is not a vague, fuzzy, philosophical ideal but a vibrant, active interchange.[5]

Such contact can produce the connection that we need to develop along the growth continuum of the psychospirituality of communion, union, ecstasy, and eternity.

It would be interesting to collect all the readers of this book in a classroom somewhere and ask each one to describe in words or pictures a portrait of a marriage or love relationship that expressed the authentic psychospirituality of communion, union, ecstasy, and eternity. What would the picture you draw look like? How would that compare with your experience and your expectation for your love relationships? Would the two pictures be similar? Would they have anything to do with the overshadowing meaning of the *spirituality of sex*, as indicated in the title of this work and described in our discussion?

Would we all be able to see the ways in which the psychospirituality (psychological meaning quest) of the growth continuum, from contact to connection, communion, union, ecstasy, and eternity, shaped either of the pictures you portrayed? What could you do to make the pictures fit that continuum more effectively? If you did that in your own life and loves, what would that look like for you and your lover? Would you like that better than the way things are for you now? Do you have the energy, courage, intelligence, and motivation to create that greater joy for yourself and your lover?

Jerry Greenwald is familiar to many people concerned with our type of discussion and the insights we have shared so far because he once published a book titled *Be the Person You Were Meant to Be.*[6] Chances are that you have read it. It was really quite popular. However, he also gave us a volume that he called *Creative Intimacy, How to Break the Patterns That Poison Your Relationships.*[7] He wrote his book to identify 11 mistakes people make in intimate relationships that cause them to miss out on the psychospirituality of true communion, union, and ecstasy because they never discover the real spirituality of sex.

The 11 patterns that poison relationship, Greenwald thinks, have to do with the following:

1. Being a timetable lover
2. Telling yourself everything is great when you are ignoring your real feelings or the tensions and frustrations in the relationship
3. Expecting the other person to make you feel whole and fulfilled
4. Preoccupation with sexual techniques and artificial turn-ons
5. Just being a superficial good sport in the relationship and never disclosing who you are and what you need or desire
6. Sharing with your lover only good things about yourself and never expressing your feelings or being truly real with him or her
7. Using love or making love as a safety valve for your fear and anxiety
8. Smothering real expression of feeling to avoid turbulence in the relationship
9. Denying to yourself and your lover that your "safe relationship" is monotonous
10. Constantly throwing up distractions that deflect the relationship from real intimacy
11. Living by the slogan of keeping it light in the relationship and never really investing yourself

Greenwald gives a cryptic summary of his book's message by suggesting that we should all develop a healthy affirmation of a relationship as it happens, while retaining the sense of when it becomes realistically necessary to terminate it. Operating on the assumption that our society is becoming increasingly impersonal, he concludes that all of us are inevitably going to feel more alone, alienated, and lost unless we can learn to build real relationships, in spite of the direction our society is going. To be alone, lonely, and isolated or alienated is toxic, says Greenwald. Adrift in the world with no relationship grounding or anchor, we lose our identity and the meaningfulness of life, as discussed throughout this book. "The most vital and most effective source of security and emotional nourishment is available within ourselves. Discovering and developing this inner strength is the primary antidote to our fears of loneliness and alienation."

That strength within ourselves is our ability to develop the kind of intimate relationships that nurture our lover and in the process nurture our own self-acceptance and self-esteem. I sense that Greenwald would agree with Jesus of Nazareth in his dictum that we should love ourselves enough that we will know what it means to love another person in the same way and to the same degree that we love ourselves. We automatically love ourselves by natural survival instinct. It is unconscious and primal.

However, it requires a conscious intentional decision if we are going to love someone else with that same instinctive depth and breadth of caring with which we love ourselves. Moreover, truly loving another requires loving that person as the person he or she really is and not as a caricature we have projected. Greenwald's book is about the variety of precarious enigmas that arise in our effort to love others as we love ourselves. His cryptic summary applies here: we should always be ready to affirm our lover, except in those matters that are false, painful, or intolerable for our own integrity and our personal value system. If we do not readily say "yes" to a lover, we are narcissistic. If we do not know when to draw the line in saying "no," we are neurotically dependent, failing to do our job of adequate and honest communication in the relationship. In the latter case we are allowing ourselves to fall into the pattern he calls "the detour lover," who denies the reality of his or her own feelings and values and paints a false picture of himself or herself for the other person.

Neither the narcissistic attitude nor the detour behavior can bring to a relationship the kind of cherishing openness in wooing and courting that must form the foundation for the growth of the psychospirituality of real communion and genuine union. The psychospirituality (meaning) of sex goes missing. Then the true richness of intimacy, sexual and spiritual, cannot develop and satisfy our irrepressible inner hunger for a meaning-filled life. A great sense of mutual satisfaction of both their needs arises for two people in love when they are able to provide each other a full sense of meaning by their intimacy. This enables each of them to accept the commitments of love to each other without feeling like it is a sacrifice or deprivation of the self in either case.

Perhaps you answered the earlier questions about the pictures of your relationship by saying to yourself that you can see areas in which you could improve things if you gathered up the courage and motivation to communicate about it. That means you are in the 60 percent of the human race who are honest and healthy. Loyalty to your lover and to yourself urges that you take whatever risks are necessary to open up your relationship to the renewal that can make it more closely reflect the authentic spiritual meaning quest that is irrepressibly present in both of you but that may have been neglected or unconsciously unattended for some time. The fruitfulness of such a renewal of the quest for profound relationship usually leads to a new sense of the spirituality (life-shaping meaning) of sex. This can produce a deepening of the meaningfulness of life as foreplay and of sexual play itself as fulfillment of our hearts longing. Sexuality was not designed just for physical release of the drives of the libido, but for cementing the spiritual (meaning), emotional, and psychological bond between two people.

Greenwald thinks the average troubled or toxic relationship can be fixed more easily than most people think. He describes a number of steps to make healing happen. One must start with developing an awareness of what each person is doing in the relationship that poisons their intimacy. Then it is important to achieve good discernment of how each person insinuates that toxic contribution into their mutual interaction. We can never see our spouse, friend, or lover really objectively, but only through the lens we have developed in our own minds and the image we have projected on them. So it is imperative that each person in the coupled relationship examine himself or herself and not get into the job of examining the other person. Sometimes a third party, such as a counselor, is necessary to help get an accurate picture of what is poisoning the relationship.

The second step is communication from both sides of the couple relationship. It takes two to tango, the old adage says, and one person cannot recreate real connection and communion if the other hangs back and hides. A couple came to me for therapy because they were both hopelessly sad about their marriage. He showed his intense concern by expressing his feelings freely, descriptively, and with a great deal of grief. Her feelings about their trouble were just as intense, I think, but she manifested them by quietly crying most of the time, with occasional outbursts of anger and accusation about how he failed to meet her expectations in marriage.

It became clear after a number of therapy sessions that he was a responsible husband who provided as well as he could for his wife and three children. She had insisted on being a stay-at-home mom. He had agreed. He tried to save money for family vacation. He gave in to her insistence that they send the children to a costly private school, though it strained the family finances to the extreme, and an excellent public school was available.

He also strongly wanted the marriage to succeed, though she spoke often of ending it. When he asked her privately and in therapy what she wanted, needed, and desired or what would resolve any of her issues, her response was always, "I don't know," or "If you do not understand on your own, it will do me no good to explain it to you," or "I need to think about it for a while." In the latter case, she would never return to the issue or tell us what she thought about it. When I addressed similar inquiries to her in therapy, her responses to me were the same as they had been to him. When I attempted to help her work through an answer to any of these questions, she exploded in angry accusations against her husband, distracting the line of thought from the issue and retreating into withdrawn silent weeping.

It turned out that her responses to him and to me were defensive strategies to protect her from exposing anything about her feelings, insights, thought processes, or expectations. Her only emotion seemed to be rage and a profound sense of loss. For a long period of therapeutic intervention, it was difficult to determine whether she suffered from cognitive impairment, overwhelming narcissism, borderline personality disorder, or dysthymia (depression). For our purposes here, what counts, of course, is the fact that here we had a couple with three children, in which family constellation he was relatively high-functioning in the ways that a husband, lover, and father needs to be. She was thoroughly dysfunctional in virtually all the ways in which a wife, lover, and mother needs to be functional.

His attempt to compensate for her deficits and carry the load of their life together on his own back, so to speak, brought no gains, and any attempt at the one thing necessary for gaining ground, namely communication, resulted in her refusing to participate. He was a player, she a hostile spectator. He communicated; she blocked all communication. Indeed, her response was consistently to counterattack in irrational and usually incoherent rage whenever he communicated with her. She clearly wanted no solutions. She simply wanted to bitch and moan and burn down the house, so to speak.

In the end, it became evident that she was suffering from a number of specific dysfunctions. First, she had a very modest IQ, to say the least. Life was, consequently, usually overwhelming for her and apparently had always been so. Her capacity for creating and working with models for efficient care of the children or management of the home was virtually nonexistent. When she got an idea in her head, such as becoming a vegetarian, sending the kids to a costly private school, being attracted by some cultish Eastern religion, or perceiving that her husband was an evil man, she became obsessive about that ideation. She was completely irrational and incoherent in her insistence on spending the money on the private school, planning costly vacations, wasting money on shopping trips every time she had access to any cash, and then attacking her husband because he did not have the money to put a new roof on the house or repair the siding.

By now you have imagined her diagnosis. She had been depressed from childhood and since puberty had manifested severe symptoms for borderline personality disorder, with particular manifestations in high levels of narcissism, obsessive-compulsiveness, chronic situation-inappropriateness, paranoia, possible bipolar depression, and reclusiveness. This is a condition that is genetic in origin and biochemically mediated and thus an inherited form of suffering. Her family history was replete with this disorder, in the severe category, going back as far as we could trace it. The carrier of the disorder was easily identifiable in each generation for the last five sets of parents, grandparents, great grandparents, and so forth.

Such suffering can be treated only by medically changing the biochemistry that causes the symptoms and dysfunction. In order to give this person a chance at participating in and contributing to a relationship of wholeness and mutuality, it was necessary to place her on a regimen of medicine for the rest of her life. Unfortunately, people who suffer from this set of disorders typically get reasonably functional in six months or so when properly medicated. Then they tend to claim they are cured and stop taking their medication. This heads them down the slippery slide into their special form of hell again. One often gets the impression that they like their misery and the drama of its hellishness more than they like stability.

Fortunately, her husband is both a bright fellow and infinitely caring. He was able to understand the situation, support the intervention, cherish his wife like one would a wounded soldier, and hope for the day in which a whole and mature relationship could be restored, and they could find the path of the psychospirituality of communion, union, and ecstasy. Their union may never be a perfect one. Who has a perfect one? But they may be able to achieve a relatively good one in which love and cherishing can help them find the spirituality of sex and the meaning of life.

Esau and Burch suggest that a union in love is a portrait of many faces. None needs to be perfect, nor do they all need to look alike. Indeed, marriages should be expected to be quite individual and different. A good marriage can be many kinds of things but will at least involve deep empathy, openness to each other, mutual valuing, sexual play, a strong desire for authenticity in the other person as well as in oneself, and loyalty. These need to be ongoing and developing processes. Style of communication, agenda of shared activities, preferred lifestyle, and a couple's choices on the division of labor in their lives depend on how the partners negotiate the differences in their preferences and expectations.

Some couples like intense activity; others like quiet reflection together. Understanding, gentleness, and shared communication between lovers will always enhance the process of building quality relationship along the road of the psychospirituality of communion, union, and ecstasy. This process is known at the deep inner level only by those who are in the actual experience of it. Thus it is important that each person take responsibility for his part in exploring all the aspects of the problems and solutions of any relationship. Greenwald assures us that "the stronger our own sense of identity, the deeper our intimacy with ourselves, the greater our potential for ... growing intimate relationship with another."[8]

From ancient times, the Western world has tended to speak of this intimate sense of mutuality between lovers as the experience of being "one flesh."

Most people are aware that this is an old term taken from the Bible. In marriage or in bonded love relationships, "these two shall become one flesh." This phrase often was interpreted as meaning that the bond of love is made up only of the fleshly connection between two people, namely, sex. That idea did a lot of damage because it tended to create a psychological outlook in which sex was sheared off from the spiritual, emotional, intellectual, psychological, and social aspects of a wholesome relationship.

It is unfortunate that this outlook led to an increasing tendency in the Christian Church over the centuries to treat sex with a negative tone and idealize the more spiritual aspects of relationship. This was tragic first because it was false and second because it made it impossible for people to think of relationship in a holistic sense. It caused the human community to make spirituality ethereal and virtually unreachable and made sex merely an appetite of the animal instincts of humans. This led to all the distorted sexual gymnastics that resulted in massive sexual abuse throughout all Western communities, most specifically by priests in the church, as we now know.

When the church and Western society relegated sex to the level of mere animal instincts and then gave those instincts a bad name and a nasty aura, sex was severely devalued. Making sex unholy and, therefore, unspeakable, instead of seeing it as a sacred and spiritual expression of God in us, forced sexual behavior underground, so to speak. Thus the effort on the part of the church and society to control sexual behavior by devaluing it caused or at least reinforced the inevitable secrecy of prostitution, child molestation, pedophilia, sexual abuse, rape, and sexual violence of all sorts. The church owes the world of humankind an enormous debt for stimulating this widespread abuse over the centuries. This is a debt that will not begin to be paid merely by million dollar settlements of the Roman Catholic Church in Europe and the Americas for the rampant pedophilia and other kinds of sexual misbehaviors by its priests.

For centuries the official devaluation of sex led humans away from the perception of real mutuality and relationship as the psychospiritual growth we can realize in mutual sexual-spiritual communion, union, and ecstasy. It made it very difficult for us to even conceptualize the notion of the spirituality of sex. It caused us to lose the sense of sex as a spiritual process and experience, in the sense of it being part of our total connection with each other that pours our souls full of the deep meaning of life and feeds our irrepressible hunger for that meaning.

Raymond Lawrence has given us two very important books dealing articulately with this problem in the history of the Church and Christian communities. The first of his sturdy works is titled *The Poisoning of Eros*,[9] and the more recent one is *Sexual Liberation, the Scandal of Christendom*.[10] Both of these should be required reading for every citizen of every country in the

Western world. His good work has done much to correct the longstanding denigration of sex, particularly by some communities of Roman Catholic Christians and by some Christian evangelicals and fundamentalists. In such circles it has often led to a two-worlds existence by these Christians: one ethereal world in which strong emphasis is laid on church life and on rigid spiritual and ethical dogma and disciplines and the other world of secretly acceding to the irrepressible "animal instincts of the flesh" and playing around in "the nasty world of sex."

Lawrence aggressively proposes a responsible revision of the negative perspective that has done so much damage in both the believing and the secular communities of our modern Western world. He points out that the negative forces in society, mainly the ancient and medieval Christian Church, had as their chief conscious goal the devaluation of the pleasure of sexual experience. The pressures this incited for repressing sexual life as normal behavior forced sexual play underground, as noted previously. Lawrence cites the data on how this increased the prominence of pornography, adultery, pedophilia, prostitution, and other forms of secretive and illicit sexual practices. Lawrence is perfectly correct in declaring that it is at once tragic and nearly hilarious that the Christian movement, with its efforts to impose restrictions on the natural and God-given needs and drives at the core of our humanness, should have instead increased the socially poisonous and personally destructive distortions of this beautiful gift of human sexuality.

The negative view of sex, and the tendency of some Christian communities and persons throughout history to shear it off from spirituality and from the full meaningfulness of life, is particularly unfortunate because the official theoretical doctrine of the Church throughout the ages has championed sex as a gift from God and as an essential part of a whole mature spirituality. In any case, the time is long overdue for us to restore to spirituality and sexuality that full-orbed meaning and unity that makes it possible for us to think again of sexuality and spirituality as two expressions of the same life force at the center of ourselves. Only then shall we be able to think in terms of the spirituality of sex which leads psychospiritually to a dynamic personal experience of relationship as sexual-spiritual connection, communion, union, ecstasy, and eternity. Let that crescendo of intensifying relationship be the joyful blossoming of every person, sexually and spiritually!

God bless our sexuality!
It was God's idea, after all.
God thought it up,
Designed its delicious dynamics.
God gave us this gift.

What a good deal, a precious gift!
God had so many other options.

God chose this one.
God lit up human life with great sex
And we screwed it up!

Can we recover God's good gift?
Unscrew the inscrutable
That we screwed up?
Can we try really cherishing love:
Find God's gift anew?

CHAPTER 6

Spirituality as Being
Really, Intimately *Present*
to Another Person

The highest level of psychospiritual gratification in sexual play and sexual union depends on the ability of persons to be really present to each other in their times of intimate relationship. Life is full of interesting distractions and responsibilities. Savoring the flavor of the spiritual dimension of sexual relationship is enhanced by sensing that each person is deeply aware of the other. That means being sensitive to the mood, emotional tone, physical moves, body language, facial expression, eye contact, and aura of longing in a lover. Being really, totally present!

In such experience of being present to and with one's lover, undistracted and sensing the lover similarly responding, one can feel the embrace of that existential process in which one's sense of time evaporates, one's sense of the surroundings is lost, and one is only aware of the wholeness of the person loving and being loved. Sexual experience as genuine presence to one's lover moves one far beyond mere mechanical sex to the meaningful emotionality and spirituality of ethereal union of body, mind, and spirit.

Theodor Reik, in *Psychology of Sex Relations*, has a chapter specifically on the topic of his book's title. In it he develops at length a commentary on the nature and importance of being present to one's lover in the sense of acknowledging the authentic person of that other human being. When two people have sex without even knowing each other, it is merely two bodies connecting and separating without any communion. Nothing has happened except two objects bumping into each other on the stage of life. What really connects two lovers is the spiritual energy generated in each of their libidos and causing their entire selves to reach out for and embrace the other. When it is not a matter of a person embracing another person with real presence to the other, it is raw, crass, and unromantic. Indeed it is the opposite of love and romance.

Reik tells a horrible story of a Frenchman who, while in Vienna to attend a Wagnerian festival, fell into conversation with an attractive young woman. He suggested that they take a walk together after the performance. Both in a romantic mood, they strolled together in the meadow in the dark. He suggested they lie down in the soft cool grass. As their inevitable sexual arousal began, she said to him breathlessly, "But Antoine, it is so dark, I cannot even see your face at all!" Antoine replied in the heights of sexual ardor, "Face—be damned." In his crude libidinal drive, her face, her individuality, her person was entirely unimportant, and only her sexual endowments meant everything. In such anonymity there is no presence of any kind to the other person. Therefore, there can be no love and no connected communion.

In love, the other person is the focus and center of the lover's universe. In such an anonymous encounter as that between Antoine and the Austrian maid, only the special foci of her body are of essential importance to the sexual event. Anonymity devalues and obviates the personality of the beloved. Raw sex is just the keen edge of biological acting out. The object of the acting out could be any anonymous human being. No particular person is of significance. In mere sex, the object can be changed. In love the beloved is not interchangeable with any other. It is said that the French king Louis XV urged his valet, "You must get me a woman. It is a matter of my biological health. It does not matter who she is. Just make sure that first you bathe her and take her to the dentist!" She might as well have been a fence post with a nice smooth hole at about the level of his hips. Women can be as anonymous in choosing partners. Reik had a patient who said to him, "I wanted him as a man, but not him as himself."[1]

Healthy persons always feel that impersonal sex is degrading. One can feel more lonely and alone in an uncongenial relationship than when one is indeed alone. Mere sex can leave both lonely. Shared love never does. In sexual play that has no real presence of one lover to another, the body might say, "Yes," but the spirit usually says, "No." The morning after, one feels jaded and may even hate oneself for the meaningless experimentation. Frequent indulgence in such anonymous sexual play usually leaves one jaded for life, with the inner spirit sheared off from the mechanical behaviors of one's acts of sexual gratification. The alternative is to make love only with a lover to whom one can be wholly present in tender cherishing: whole person to whole person in foreplay, communion, union, and climax. The goal is real presence.

Leslie Karen Lobell asks pointedly on her Web page,[2]

Do you show up—I mean really show up—when you have sex or make love? You might think, "Well, anyone would show up for that, right?" In the past, I would have agreed with this statement. Now, I have some serious doubts. . . . Being present is essential to creating a full, sensuous, enjoyable experience of life. . . . Few people realize how little time they spend being present . . . even for events that should be pleasurable.

I used to think . . . that I showed up all the time. Then, in my early thirties, I received a "wake up call" when I began to do a lot of "consciousness work" . . . this was an intensive new phase of my personal growth process, bringing a whole new level of self-discovery. . . . The more I learned about becoming aware and being present, the more I realized how little time I had been spending . . . in the present. I once had . . . the embarrassing realization that . . . whenever I was making love I would suddenly transport myself, mentally, to places I had been before. Without any warning or logical connection to anything, my mind would take me to a square in Florence, a house in Greece, an outdoor hot-tub in Arizona, or a cliff overlooking the Pacific Ocean in California.

In order to have a heightened, sensual experience, you really need to get present. . . . you cannot have a fully embodied, "blow your mind and curl your toenails" kind of orgasm when your mind is wandering off somewhere. Neither can you build deep intimacy with a romantic partner under such circumstances, if that is what you are seeking to do. Do you show up for the "Big O"?

Lobell thinks we ought to ask ourselves whether we are really experiencing the person we are with or are simply comparing the present lover with a previous one. We should be aware of whether we are really making love with *this* person or fantasizing about some other scene, person, or experience. If I am watching a sunset or driving in the mountains with someone I love, is it a truly sharing experience, or am I thinking how nice it would be if I were there with a different person, or if I were in a different place just then? Am I present in that moment and experience or worrying about getting somewhere else to do something else? Am I experiencing the moment or worried about finding a gas station? Am I present or "checked out," as Lobell puts it?

As I have implied in the previous paragraph, and as Lobell also suggests, being truly present is an opportunity for relationship and personal inspiration in most any setting in life, not just in sexual play or orgasm.

If you discover . . . that you are not present very often . . . that can serve as a wake up call . . . to bring yourself back to the present. Many of us avoid the present. When we are in the present, . . . we feel vulnerable to life, and . . . pain. However, it is only in taking the risk of being present that we can experience sheer joy and ecstasy, as well. So, the next time . . . take a risk: Show up for the "Big O"! You'll be glad you came![3]

Lobell's question applies to all aspects of life in which we have the opportunity for relationship of any kind. It applies to intellectual conversations; to emotional events in which we can or must share an experience of our own or of another; and when either of us is sad, mad, glad, or scared. Be present! Her question applies equally when we are sharing a surprising or awesome aesthetic experience of some natural or created beauty, watching a sunset, viewing a Rembrandt, worshipping together, celebrating together, studying together, or sharing a psychological, social, or spiritual experience.

Julienne is married to Harvey. He was previously married to Marie, with whom he has four children. Julienne came to me sad and confused because she felt, after two years of marriage, that Harvey was never really present in their relationship. He had a good job as a corporate vice president, made a superb salary, and provided a delightful lifestyle for them. She was a teaching consultant to the public school systems of a major metropolitan area. He worked long hours and was frequently out of town on business, but had relatively good control of his own schedule and could adapt his time relatively well to family needs.

Harvey was an absolutely devoted father. He had been divorced from Marie for six years, and the children were now all busy teenagers. The children all had a good relationship with Harvey. What grieved and often exasperated Julienne was mainly the fact that it seemed to her that anytime Marie called her or Harvey to assist in a special need of the children, Harvey was quick to respond and fill that need. This took much time and energy from her relationship with him. The children were with Harvey and Julienne every other weekend from Friday to Monday and at least one overnight during every week. That amounted to a great deal of time with the children. Julienne was not disturbed by that. She was disturbed by the fact that during Marie's time with the children, something regularly came up for which Marie required Harvey's or Julienne's help.

Sometimes it was a matter of taking a child to a doctor's appointment, ball game, hockey practice, or any inadvertency that happened to conflict with Marie's sudden whim to get a hair appointment or have a drink with a friend. Julienne liked the children and loved Harvey. However, it seemed to her that Marie was constantly setting the agenda of Harvey's relationship with Julienne with these impositions. These events were always scheduled for the children by Marie and constantly took major amounts of time away from Julienne's and Harvey's time together. In fact, it seemed to her that anytime the children informed Marie that Harvey and Julienne had special plans, Marie called to ask Harvey to take the kids for some reason. Harvey always complied. Sometimes Julienne concluded that their special times were intentionally torpedoed by Marie.

It had gotten to the point that Julienne was developing the impression that although Harvey had divorced Marie six years ago and married Julienne two years ago, he had never really left the relationship with Marie and the children as the primary relationship constellation in his life. She felt he was more readily present to Marie than he was to her. She desperately wanted her relationship with him to be clearly the primary relationship constellation in his life. She was, of course, quite right in her expectation and hope. Julienne is a wise, kind, and constructive woman. She had nothing against Marie as a person but felt, quite correctly, that her husband was never really present to her in any aspects of their lives.

Very busy with his work and devoted to his children, he constantly refused to confront Marie about anything regarding the children. Marie's passive-aggressive control of his life was the reason he had divorced her. If he tried to confront her about anything that she demanded, it would backfire, with her informing the children that their father refused to look after their needs and did not really care about them. When he married Julienne, Marie expressed this kind of destructive diatribe to the children with some intensity. She informed the children that their father cared more for his "new whore" than for them. Harvey was caught between his passion for his children's well-being during their developing years and his difficulty in extricating himself from Marie's castrating control, in order to invest himself without reservation in his relationship with Julienne.

Julienne's perception was precisely accurate. The net result of Harvey's predicament was that he was never permitted by Marie to be really present to Julienne or to make his relationship with her the primary relationship constellation in his life, at least so far as the expenditure of his time and energy was concerned. What made the situation worse instead of better, surprisingly, was the fact that during Harvey and Julienne's courtship, of which Marie had no knowledge, they had a truly glorious relationship of real and intense presence to each other. It was a relationship like neither Julienne nor Harvey had ever known or heard about. Moreover, whenever they did get a few moments of real time together now, Julienne could still see glimpses of that early profound relationship. She rightfully longed to have it back.

Paying genuine attention to the other person is the most complete gift of ourselves we are able to offer anyone in this life. To give our spouse, friend, or lover that kind of attention involves letting our consciousness be completely given over to that other person. That means that when we are with our lover, we set aside all thoughts about what we would rather be doing, where we would rather be, with whom we would prefer to spend the time, what duty we should be attending, whether the children need us, or whether an assignment will be late.

To be fully present to our lover even means that we are not thinking about what we want from this relationship, what we ought to be saying, or how we ought to be moving just now. It means to have moved past our analytic left brain and to have entered wholly into right-brain function where our affective world and our unconscious can lead us into the natural moves, emotions, and expressions in which we savor the flavor of the beauty, gratification, and utter fulfillment of this season of intense union with that special other person.

In his fine book, *The Origin of Consciousness in the Breakdown of the Bicameral Mind,* Julian Jaynes has informed us that our most meaningful experience of life is not derived from our analytical and logical consciousness. That is important left-brain work. However, the meaningfulness of our lives derives mostly from our right brain, in which we experience our emotional, aesthetic, and intuitive meanings.[4] There we sense the meaning of life through its texture, color, beauty, artistic qualities, relationality, sensations, ESP, prescience, and intuition. There we also find our experience of the ethereal, transcendent, and divine world. Jaynes is quite sure that the ancient biblical prophets experienced their remarkable insights into the meaning of life and the prospects of the future from the parapsychological function of their right brains. In their right brains they heard the voice of God.

Do you suppose that is the reason everybody all around the world tends to cry out, "Oh God!" while experiencing orgasm? Surely that level of intensity and intimacy forms an event in which we have set all conscious awareness aside and have transcended our circumstance, our time, and ourselves. Indeed, it is a moment divine! Who would ever say otherwise? That is why I feel sorry for atheists. Their most unfortunate problem is that they have no one to call out to while having an orgasm. On the other side of the coin, so to speak, a few weeks ago my deacon put the following quip on our church sign: "It does not count as church attendance to lie in bed on Sunday morning, crying out, 'Oh God! Oh God!'"

The experience of being truly present to one's lover may vary in length of time. It really has nothing to do with whether much or little time is available for an experience with another person. As noted in previous chapters, life is foreplay, and on any given day the season of intense presence may last from dawn to dusk, so to speak, or may be a genuinely loving investment of emotion in an enveloping kiss as one rushes out the door in the morning, late to catch the train. It may begin as lovers meet for an evening and last through long conversation, a pleasant meal, a shared entertainment, and the experience of making love. Or it may be the intense, even hurried, lovemaking at lunch when one has escaped briefly from work in desperate desire to share a few intense moments with one's true love.

At the Catholic girls' high school that my daughter attended, one of the Sisters of Mercy conducted a fine informative class on human sexuality. She concluded it appropriately with the caution that the adolescent students should avoid promiscuous sex and at least protect themselves against pregnancy. She wisely observed that if they failed to do that, they might find that for an hour of fun, they would have a life time of misery. Promptly one of the girls in the back of the room raised her hand and asked, "Sister, would you tell us how to make it last an hour?"

Regardless of the length of time, what counts is the quality of the presence during that time. To be truly present and attend to a lover is to be empty of one's own project for that season of love. Being genuinely present is not just making a place in my awareness for my lover. It is to turn my awareness over to my lover, to be generously solicitous in the fullest possible way.[5] Thus, presence to my lover means more than just "getting my rocks off." It means being there because of an irrepressible desire to give my lover the experience of that gratification and sense of wholeness and fullness that comes only through real connection, deep communion, genuine union, and indescribable ecstasy. I want to give her the feeling that she has reached the top of a mountain of meaning and found a grand vista of life as a new person.

Harvey will never be able to do that for Julienne or allow her to do it for him if Marie is always perched on his shoulder, ready to set his agenda for the next moment or the next move. Julienne has a right and need to require that the primary relationship constellation in Harvey's life be his family with her, not his family with Marie. That is a tricky trajectory for Harvey unless he can create an adequate understanding with his now maturing children in which he enlists them in the project of protecting his life with Julienne without feeling that he is neglecting them. If he can engage the children in that kind of understanding, thus disempowering Marie in her efforts to manipulate his life, he can finally be free to love his children appropriately, be really present to Julienne, and finally really divorce himself from Marie.

Then Harvey will be free to give Julienne that mountaintop experience of real presence—and notice the same from her. Such a moment can be for both like the parting of the veil that normally blinds us to the transcendent spiritual (meaning) world of union beyond our ordinary selves. That is a world where for a season we feel whole and completely our meaning-filled selves. Such an experience of mutuality shows us that our ordinary, everyday taken-for-granted reality is not the whole of reality and perhaps not even the most real of our potential experiences of reality.[6] Indeed, to achieve authentic communion, union, and ecstasy with a lover is to achieve a genuine altered state, produced by the most central and normal of all human experiences, real presence in sexual play. That altered state is spirituality in full bloom, spirituality as defined throughout this book, the irrepressible inner human hunger and quest for life-fulfilling meaning, fulfilled at last. I suppose that is why Oprah is said to have declared, "Being truly present is heaven!"

The late Henri Nouwen was a Catholic priest and professor at Yale University. He wrote many lovely books about the spirituality of human relationships. Many of us remember him most for his striking little work titled *The Wounded Healer*.[7] In his earlier book simply titled *Intimacy*, he inquired whether that intense love and the kind of relationship Oprah refers to can really be achieved by us. He asks, "Is love a utopian dream or a possibility within our reach?" He seems quite sure that the story of human relationship is such that "there is a spark of misunderstanding in every intimate encounter, a painful experience of separateness in every attempt to unite, a fearful resistance in every act of surrender."[8]

As boldly as he asks his question, Nouwen answers it. Although it is true that too many of the most noticeable aspects of relationship in our lives have to do with control and manipulation, giving and forgiving are the forms of intimacy that keep life and love alive in all the undercurrents of civilized existence. Some folks are genuinely suspicious that the reality we call love is just a blanket to cover the real fact that relationships are about conquest and subtle or overt power. The difference between relationships of power and relationships of love is the quality of giving rather than taking that comes spontaneously and naturally from the soul of each lover. Nouwen strongly emphasizes that love is giving ourselves to our lovers and keeping our selves open to freely receive the same from them, rather than setting standards of judgment about how they should relate to us.

Love, in this mode, is a spirit of acceptance that reaches out and embraces our lovers, full of forgiveness for any human lack or difference in expectation from what we wished for or anticipated. Acceptance and forgiveness are the components of true love in Nouwen's view. "Love means openness, vulnerability, availability, and confession" of our human limitations and the real nature of our selves. Love is a kind of giving that allows the lover to show his or her real self in all its strengths and weaknesses, beauty and inadequacy, cleverness and stumbling. Love is a possibility. All of us need to go through the process of learning that it is safe to love, that love is our only chance at a real, full life. That begins with our acceptance of our own *humanness* and that of our lovers.

Nouwen thinks that it is much easier to learn to love freely and fully if we have a deep sense that we are unconditionally loved, accepted, and forgiven by God. Then, he says, we will own a deep inner sense that it is safe to embrace our own vulnerability because we know that we are in loving hands. It is safe to be available to our lovers because we stand on the solid ground of knowing our vulnerability and humanness is acceptable and will not be held against us. It is then safe to surrender to a lover because we know we will not fall into a dark pit but always will enter into the welcoming home of the lover's embrace and care. It is safe to be weak, inadequate, and flawed because we are invited by the creative desire of our lovers into real human communion and union.[9]

To live this way is a new way of knowing. We are surrounded not by the darkness of fear and shame, but by the light of love. If we have experienced this light, we will know what this means. Acceptance and forgiveness are so intimate a part of this because they are the acts that open the gates of love in both directions, from lover to lover. "Maybe we remember the few occasions in our life in which we were able to show someone we love our real self: not only our great successes but also our weaknesses and pains, not only our good intentions but also our bitter motives, not only our radiant face but also our dark shadow. It takes a lot of courage, but it might just open a new horizon, a new way of living."[10]

The new world this opens to us offers a new sense of certainty, never before experienced in quite the same way. It assures us that peace, forgiveness, goodness, justice, and inner freedom are more than mere words. They amount to a conversion of our lives that clarifies that real love is a genuine possibility. Love then is not a clinging to each other in the fear of not being accepted and loved, but an encounter in a freedom that allows for the creation of a new way of living together. We are invited to such love and find it to be safe and healing by offering our own engaging response to it.[11]

Nouwen emphasized that "love is based on the mutuality of the confession of our total self to each other. This makes us free . . . When the exposure of one's deepest dependency becomes an invitation to share this most existential experience we enter a new area of life."[12] This is what Oprah can call an experience of heaven. This love is truthful, tender, and disarming. "When the physical encounter of men and women in the intimate act of intercourse is not an expression of their total availability to each other, the creative fellowship . . . is not yet reached."[13]

Nouwen completes these thoughts with what should be a classic quote from his life's work:

> Love is limitless. Only when men and women give themselves to each other in total surrender, that is, with their whole person for their whole life, can their encounter bear full fruits. When through the careful growth of their relationship men and women have come to the freedom of total disarmament, their giving also becomes for-giving, their nakedness does not evoke shame but desire to share, and their ultimate vulnerability becomes the core of their mutual strength. (32)

When one looks at things in this way, it is clear that the sexual act is an act of spirituality.

When I published my previous book on sexuality, *Sex in the Bible*, I overheard a fellow browsing in a bookstore exclaim in horror, "How could he use 'Sex' and the 'Bible' in the same sentence?!" I walked over to him and had a nice chat. It became clear rather quickly that it was not some religious scruple in him that had given rise to his shock. He proved to be a thoroughly secular person who could not imagine having anything to do with God or ever darkening the door of a church, synagogue, or mosque. I was struck by the fact that this irreligious, secular citizen was so split in his inner self that even he, who should hardly care what I do with God or religion, could not tolerate my connecting God with human sexuality. I suspect that his problem was not a fear that I would thereby desecrate God. Rather, I think he did not want me to desecrate his view of sex by suggesting that it may have moral or spiritual facets and implications.

Looking at the spirituality of our intimate presence to each other in the outlook we have been cultivating so far confirms Nouwen's, Oprah's, and Merton's perspectives. In the past, religion and sexuality have so often been described as opponents. In this new perspective they "merge into one and the same reality when they are seen as an expression" of the total giving of one's self to another human being.[14] That is a God-like thing to do.

Of course, as stated or alluded to already, being really present to another human can be an experience at the intellectual, social, psychological, emotional, and spiritual levels as well as at the sexual level. Real presence may involve any or all of these aspects of intimacy. A complete and real presence means connection at all six levels. However, when we are truly present to another person at any of these levels, we are always aware, often acutely aware, of that other person's sexuality and of our own. Sexuality and spirituality are inseparable. Experiencing meaningful relationship involves real awareness of the spirituality of sex and the sexuality of our spirituality. In the cultivation of quality and constructive development of any relationship, it is critically important to be clear on where the boundaries ought to be for the expression of both our sexuality and our spirituality (our shared meaning).

Instinctive sexual and spiritual attraction is the primary driver of our desire to be truly present to another human being at any or all of the six levels. Therefore it is crucial to know to what extent intimacy at any or all those levels is constructive or destructive for any given relationship. To set limits on the sexual union may enhance the communion and union and the true presence, on the intellectual, social, or spiritual level. That depends on the kind of relationship this particular one is supposed to be. Intellectual and social intimacy with a faculty colleague is one kind of relationship. Spiritual and emotional intimacy with a person in one's prayer group is another kind of relationship. Mutual appreciation between one's self and a neighbor is another kind of relationship.

It is possible, even necessary or desirable, to be intimately present in any or all of these three relationships and to be fully aware of the sexual energy evident in all of them on both sides. However, it is also important to realize that acting on that energy to share sexual intimacy, particularly intercourse, will likely spoil some important aspects of the primary nature of the particular kind of relationship this one is: neighbor, colleague, or prayer group partner. Nonetheless, all of these relationships will profit from our being really present in them. In any of these intimate relationships, sexual attraction is the primary and most powerful feature of love. Of course, we must constantly decide in which of our relationships it is appropriate to express this sexual level of our real presence to each other.

When allowed free course in an appropriate setting, this sexual attraction will ensure the union of those who are sexually compatible. However, this intense attraction, a profound experience of real presence to each other, and sexual compatibility are not an adequate basis or assurance of a true, fruitful, and enduring love experience or a successful marriage. That requires the additional commitment to work together to discover the way to full enmeshment of two lives at all six levels of presence to, and pouring one's self out for, the other.

Perhaps the ancient Greeks understood better than any of us since then the ways in which love prompts real presence to each other in our relationships, thus forming true intimacy. They realized how many different things people mean by the word *love*. In English we really have only one word for love. We can use such additional words as affection, cherishing care, longing, and the like, but those all get defined again by the term *love*, and we are unclear exactly what we mean by those additional words. To understand what we mean by them, we need to take note of the context in the rest of the sentence, and in that way we discover that what is meant by them is some expression of love.

The ancient Greeks had three words for love: *filia, eros*, and *agape*. Each had a very distinctive meaning, which helps us here in clarifying what we mean by the kind of love that is truly present to another person. *Filia* was a word the ancients used to describe the relationship of friendship or brotherly love. By that word they meant the kind of caring interaction between two friends in which both contributed much giving to the shared friendship, and both received a lot from it. To have a filial relationship with another person meant that you could count on the relationship to contribute some genuine good to your own life, and you expected to contribute something of value to the life of your friend. The good that both could be counted on to bring to and get from the relationship could be something material, psychological, social, or spiritual. In any case, the reason to be in the relationship was that you got from it a lot of what you wanted and needed in a friend, and you could respond in kind as appropriate.

The ancient Greek word *eros* described a type of acquisitive desire. With this kind of love, one established a relationship strictly for what one could get out of it. We get the term *erotic* from this ancient word. *Eros* and *erotic* refer to the experience of a desire to possess something. You may have a desire to own the exotic porcelain vase from the Ming Dynasty of China that you saw in an art store. That means that you love it erotically. You wish to possess it. Likewise, you may desire to experience a good "roll in the hay" with the gorgeous person who lives next door to you. You have an intense erotic love for that person. You wish to possess him or her. If you long to see a sunset like the one you saw last fall right after a tornado storm, you are experiencing a desire to possess again, to own for just a few minutes, that aesthetic moment.

You say to your friend, "I would really love to see that again," or even, "I really long to see that again." That longing is erotic love.

It is a kind of tragedy that in our time, the word *erotic* has been so limited in popular street language because it now means almost only something sexual. Someone reads a *Playboy* magazine or *Playgirl* magazine, looking at the pictures attentively, appreciating the exotic beauty of the models, and we say that is erotic. Yes, it is, in the same sense as your desire for the sunset and mine for the Ming porcelain. We love it erotically; we desire to possess it. It was wise for the Greeks to separate out from each other these deep inner expressions of wholesome longing that are inherent to the human heart and human spirituality, a central part of our hunger for meaning.

The third word in ancient Greek for love was *agape*. It is interesting that in Modern Greek *agape* now means what *eros* meant in ancient Greece. If you say to a Greek person today that you wish to love him or her in an agapic way, he or she will believe that you wish to have sexual intercourse. However, in the ancient world and the world of the Bible, for example, *agape* meant something quite different and quite wonderful. It referred to the kind of love that pours out of itself everything that will make the object of that love more complete, beautiful, secure, and generally blessed, so to speak. Agape is the kind of love that we have been discussing throughout this book. It is love that may refer to things as well as persons, but it is usually and best used to express our relationship to another person whom we profoundly cherish.

I might say, for example, that I would love to have that Ming vase. If I simply desire to own it, that is erotic love for the vase. If I would love to have it so that I could take it and repair all the cracks that someone has carelessly put into its porcelain, spoiling it, and I wish to restore it to its original pristine beauty at my own great expense, that is agapic love. Thus, *agape* is a word we usually employ when describing our love for another person about whom we care so much that we wish to pour into him or her such great benefits, even at our own great expense, as to enhance his or her life significantly. Agapic love is the love that prompts one to be so profoundly present to one's lover or beloved that it fills that person's life with goodness.

There is a remarkable poem describing this dimension of the spirituality of sex, which manifests itself in the spirituality of being really intimately present to another person.

> This love of which I speak
> Is slow to lose patience.
> It looks for a way of being constructive
> It is not possessive.
> It is neither anxious to impress
> Nor does it cherish inflated ideas
> Of its own importance.
> Love has good manners.

Love does not pursue selfish advantage.
It is not touchy.
It does not keep account of failings
Nor does it gloat over the humanness
Of the other person.
On the contrary, it is glad
With all good folk
When truth prevails.

Love knows no limit to its endurance,
No end to its trust,
No fading of its hope.
It can outlast anything.
It is, in fact, the one thing
That still stands
When every thing else
Has fallen to pieces.[15]

D. S. Bailey took this kind of love so seriously in both its spiritual and sexual expression that he urged great frequency for this intimate total presence of lovers to each other. He described the relationship as a sacrament in which two lovers pour out of themselves and into their beloved all their healing and filling energies and passions. This total union and communion on all six levels of intimacy fills and heals both. Moreover, the frequency is important because this is the means by which lovers continually reconfirm their original union as a true oneness that continues through time and life. In this one-flesh union and communion, both are nourished and strengthened, when it is a free giving of each to the other. Bailey believes that if this quality of presence, each to the other, is achieved early in the relationship and carefully cultivated, it will last at all six levels of intimacy long after age and biochemistry have passed the point of fertility. The intimacy will still be remembered in its deep meaning and will be continued.[16]

Thomas Moore has approached this aspect of the spirituality of really being present to another human by means of the term *soul mate:*

A soul mate is someone to whom we feel profoundly connected, as though the communicating and communing that take place between us were not the product of intentional efforts, but rather a divine grace. This kind of relationship is so important . . . that many have said that there is nothing more precious in life. We may find a soul partner in many different forms of relationship—in friendship, marriage, work, play, and family. It is a rare form of intimacy . . . not limited . . . to one form.[17]

By "soul," Moore means the central self of a human being, which is deeper than the function of our will or thought or feeling. It is the life force in our conscious and unconscious spirit that causes us to value some things, experiences, and persons, indeed to attach our selves almost addictively to them and not to others. For Moore, the soul has its own reasons, and we have little access to just why they are what they are, but we need to value them highly, that is, take them seriously, in any case. Being truly present to another person is a union of persons that comes from "an attraction and magnetism of souls. . . . It is as though souls recognize the hidden treasure in each other and forge the alliance."[18]

Every once in a while, as Moore cites, we hear someone say that his or her spouse is also a best friend. That person means that the spouse is an intimate delight as spouse but also that special additional qualities bless the relationship in the form of a high degree of mutual understanding. That is a deep experience of each being truly present to the other. Such presence includes most often a "common concern for each other as individuals, and perhaps a sensitivity to the soul-work of the other," the deep inner growth, self-realization, and maturity of the other. Moore thinks this kind of presence to each other "may be the most soulful relationship, because the outer structures that bind people together are less important to the soul than its own deeply experienced life."[19]

Every relationship is a union of souls at some level. It is always spiritual and sexual at the same time. Which we explore more deeply depends on the boundaries of that particular relationship. However, each is a gift that incites some new growth in the other, in the connection, and in ourselves. From this growth comes a deeper and broader and more complete revelation to us of the inner depth of the beloved, the inner depth of our own souls, and the inner depth of the meaning of being genuinely present in every intimacy.

Presence,
Not forever staring into your eyes
Though they do seem windows to your lovely soul.

Real presence,
Far less anxious and deeply incomplete
Because you are really right here next to me.

Deep presence,
As though I feel you quite inside of me
And am profoundly comforted and fulfilled.

Your presence,
Looking forward down life's road together
Knowing that now everything is quite ok.

The Presence,
The veil between us is quite permeable
As that twixt now and God, twixt us and heaven.

CHAPTER 7

ORGASM AS SPIRITUAL EXPERIENCE

Orgasm is an abandonment of self to the experience of transcending one's self. Viewed strictly physiologically, an orgasm, like a sneeze, is a neurological and muscular spasm. It has some of the characteristics of a seizure. We lose a few brain cells every time we sneeze and every time we orgasm. What a way to go! Some people know nothing about sex except the physical animality of arousal and orgasm. That is a wonderful part of human sexuality, but these individuals' sexual play is mere sexual gymnastics, sheared off from authentic psychospiritual investment in their lover.

Masturbation is a form of sexual gymnastics that also always leaves one with a certain sense of release and relief from the internal pressures of sexual arousal but always leaves one with a profound sense of emptiness as well. That is because our sexual longing and its fulfillment have a built-in spiritual dimension, that is, the hunger for union with another person, a lover. Similarly, casual sex can be gratifying at the level of release and relief of arousal and its needs, but it leaves one empty of the meaning that healthy people long for in true relationship.

As an experience of self-transcendence, an orgasm is a moment in which a person utterly abandons all awareness of self, focus on self, and control of self. It is a moment of great risk when one freely, and with complete abandon, gives oneself wholly to one's lover, pours one's whole self out for one's lover, without any consideration of holding back. Orgasm is a sub-volitional, sub-cognitive, sub-conscious experience. Those large Latinized words mean that an orgasm is not an experience that depends on our willing it. It happens at such a deep visceral level in us that when arousal reaches the climax of intensity, our willing or not willing an orgasm has nothing to do with making it happen or not happen. It takes on a life of its own, and we have no option but to give ourselves wholly to it and, in that release of all control, to give ourselves without reservation to our lover. All energy is then focused on our lover. Our entire being—body, mind, and spirit—is irretrievably caught up in pouring ourselves out completely upon our lover.

Therefore, orgasm is the ultimate experience of the spirituality of sex. It is a spiritual experience in that it has its entire meaning in this agapic expending of ourselves for our lover. It is, in that sense, not only a spasm of self-transcendence, but a process of spiritual transcendence, namely, an experience in which our wholeness is finally realized by giving up all narcissistic self-preoccupation and giving our entire self away. We become our whole selves by expending our whole selves for another. Orgasm is the ultimate symbol of what life is about: radical and unreserved *agape!*

It is for this very reason, of course, that mere masturbation and the superficial experience of casual sex leaves one so empty and un-whole and incomplete. It is a substitute for the authentic spirituality of sex. It feels somewhat like self-transcendence, but it is wholly narcissistic and remains self-preoccupied. When the release comes at the climax of arousal, it gives release and relief but no fulfillment, no completeness. The feeling of emptiness continues, and the experience somehow increases one's profound sense of aloneness, loneliness, and isolation. We were made for communion and union as the setting for experiences of ecstasy. When we achieve orgasm without communion and union with an authentic lover, the ecstasy that we seem to feel is fake. We know it at the center of our souls, if we have not so jaded ourselves as to have long corroded the true meaning-hunger of our spirits.

I am pleased to say simply that for me, as a man, the experience of foreplay is a joyful delight. Lovemaking is an intense and exciting arousal. It feels like I am a fairly fragile ship making its way out of the heavy seas of life into an inviting haven of pleasant tranquility. As making love moves to the warmth and tenderness of penetration, it feels like my ship is finally coming into the harbor. When arousal blossoms in climax, and orgasm pours itself out to my lover, it feels like I have come home at last. All is safe and sound and secure, every need and desire is complete, every longed for expectation embraced.

If you have ever read the story of Odysseus in Homer's *Odyssey*, you can readily see how it is a metaphor for foreplay, lovemaking, and orgasm. Home at last. Home at last. The hero is home from the hunt, the victor home from the war. For me, orgasm is to be finally wholly at home, peaceful, complete, and safe from this wearying world of work and worry. It is my ultimate homecoming gift to my lover. A ship in the harbor! A wounded warrior home! An emptiness filled! A hunger fed! Giving all and unexpectedly receiving all. A joy unspeakable, indeed!

I ask my women colleagues and friends what the experience is like for them. I always wonder whether it is quite similar or very different. The very nature of the physiology of penises and vaginas must make a discernable difference in the nature of the experience. As I said, for me penetration and orgasm feel like a homecoming, entering the haven, and my women friends tell me that for them it is the experience of being totally taken up by the sensation and completely filled to satisfaction. It gives them the sense that all is well, and all is in order. The expected ship has found its haven and is home. They tell me that with a really cherished lover, the experience of being penetrated is like a feeding of a long harbored hunger, the filling of an enduring emptiness, the dissipation of a gnawing vacuum, the resolution of life's urges toward the meaning of things.

Women tend to agree with me that orgasm brings answers to questions we did not know that we were asking, resolves impasses we did not know we were facing, connects us at levels at which we did not know we were disconnected. All this takes place at the subconscious emotional level, even at the visceral level in our center. It leaves us feeling depleted and completed at the some time. Love with a true lover, consummated in an outpouring orgasm, brings a kind of ultimate peace.

Pity those poor souls who have substituted the triviality of casual sex for the cherishing of an authentic lover, or who must resort to autoeroticism, masturbation, instead of cherishing communion and union! Many folks in our day and age are sexually sophisticated but not sexually mature. Alexander Lowen believes that the restrictions on sexual freedom in the first half of the twentieth century were left over from the Victorian Age of the nineteenth century.[1] Those restrictions cramped normal, healthy openness in sexual expression and behavior. Our reaction to that during the last half century, with its cultural rebellion against all limitation, has resulted in a great deal of sexual information and experimentation in our Western world.

Unfortunately, that increase in sexual knowledge and experience has left most people sexually sophisticated but not sexually mature. Lowen says that most people today know a lot more about sexual matters than their ancestors did, but the knowledge has led more toward confusion of sexual roles and uncertainty about personal sexual goals than toward meaningful relationships.[2] The improvement in the knowledge and experience level has not relieved the average person's burden of guilt and frustration. Sexual opportunities abound in our society, but they do not seem to be bringing people generally to the joy and satisfaction that profound love holds out there for us.

"How-to" manuals fill the shelves of bookstores and sex shops. Online sources are infinite and beyond one's limitations of time and energy. Anyone who wishes to know anything can find out anything almost anywhere, and can do it in privacy if he or she insists. Exotic sexual techniques of the Eastern and Western worlds are touted everywhere. Nothing is any longer beyond the reach of anyone, even children and adolescents. All this seems to add nothing to sexual health and happiness today, if the records of any clinician are reviewed, or if any popular poll about sexual function and fulfillment can be believed. Sexual sophistication—that is, knowing a lot about all kinds of techniques and methods for sexual play—does not seem to be affording any degree of sexual maturity and might very well be producing the opposite. It seems to be producing jaded attitudes toward sexuality and cynicism about its enduring fulfillments.

Lowen observes that sexual affairs are discussed openly these days. However, enormous ignorance and misinformation saturate our culture regarding the nature and function of sexual orgasm.

> One suspects that the current sexual sophistication is a cloak that covers and hides the sexual immaturity, conflicts, and anxieties of the wearer. The popular response to books that offer the "secret" of sexual fulfillment in a few easy lessons betrays a widespread immaturity and naiveté'. The "How to Do It" books and the "How to be Happy" books would be ludicrous if the sexual situation were less desperate. As it is, they distort the problem and in the end confuse the reader.[3]

One might add that they make things much worse because such manuals always propose a number of specific steps for behavior and progress. Unfortunately, the steps do not work and never worked for the writer of those manuals either. As a result, these books create a world of fictional solutions, leaving the reader all the more frustrated and defeated because he or she feels failure, thus falling into a deeper sense of dysfunction and inadequacy. Most of us who are not flaming narcissists are somewhat neurotic; that is, our level of worry about sexual function or performance is somewhat larger than life. We have no one else with whom to compare ourselves, given that few wish to talk honestly about these things or know how to do so. As a result, we resort to the "How to Do It" manuals that make us feel like even greater failures than we originally thought, deepening our neurotic sense of self-denigration and diminishment. That, in turns, makes any sexual limitation infinitely worse. This becomes a vicious circle.

As I have emphasized throughout this volume, sexuality is a spiritual dimension of human beings. Orgasm is a spiritual experience. That means that it is an outpouring of the whole person to invest our ultimate gift of ourselves in the one we love, and it turns out that it is in precisely this season of union and ecstasy that we are filled with the transcendent meaning of our lives. That is why sexual behavior is inherently integrated into our core personality. It is an expression and function of our personalities. If our personality is dysfunctional, our sexuality cannot be healed unless our personality is healed. Sexual dysfunction always represents an impairment or pathology in the personality. If the narcissist cannot pour himself or herself out for the lover in the ecstasy of orgasm, it is not because he or she has lousy sexual technique. It is because there is a sickness in his or her personality.

Sexuality, in turn, "informs and shapes the personality."[4] That is why, as mentioned, not only do sex manuals not help much or at all, but they can even be counterproductive and defeating. Sexual fulfillment is a product of the way of life of real sexual maturity. This requires a mature personality. All this is another way of saying that sexuality is a function of our spirituality, and spirituality is a function of our sexuality. Sexual sophistication is merely clever skillfulness in the mechanics of sex, which fails to see this spiritual dimension and thus misses the connection between the body and the spirit. A sexually sophisticated person knows everything about everything sexual, but sex is all in his or her head.

That means that sex is a matter of illusion. It is some imagined experience or ideal, rather than a sense of the reality of real relationship. This person's expectations and anticipations regarding sex are mainly fanciful and not the imagined connection of real union and communion. Therefore, the ecstasy of orgasm will be fake, not a fulfilling and gratifying expending of oneself for one's lover. The same personality dysfunctions cause both emotional and sexual problems.

The sexually mature person is not a mere performer, but his or her sexual behavior is a spontaneous and natural expression of his or her real feelings. He or she is not wandering in an ethereal world of mere ideals and pretension. He or she is not preoccupied with success or failure—or some kind of perfection in the experience. This mature person knows that sexual satisfaction cannot be divorced from life-satisfaction in which a person's maturity expresses itself in a realistic and wholehearted commitment to the meaning of one's life and one's lover.

Some folks think that they can be very effective in their personality function in daily relations even if they are dysfunctional in their intimate relationships. Lowen strongly disagrees. He offers an interesting illustration:

> My experience is that people are not so split, despite their efforts to convince others and themselves that they are. Despite a common attempt to create the impression that one can function differently on these two levels, the fact is that the compulsive housewife is not a [seductive] little nighttime moth, nor is the [controlling] executive a dashing Lothario. When it comes to the sexual response, the compulsive housewife is afraid to let go, and the [controlling] executive is afraid to pour himself or herself out for his or her lover. It is my contention that the sexual behavior of a person reflects his personality, just as the personality of an individual is an expression of his sexual feelings; . . . the sexual behavior of an individual can be understood only by reference to his personality.[5]

It seems quite important that a person discern whether he or she tends toward the naive, sophisticated, or mature personality in life and love because that awareness will directly affect the effectiveness of his or her function in making love and savoring ecstatic orgasm as spiritual experience.

In our present culture it is hardly forgivable to be naive, considering that there is now so much opportunity to know a great deal about human sexuality and also much opportunity almost everywhere for wholesome sexual experimentation and exploration with trusted friends and lovers. All of us start out naive. I remember vividly how difficult it was for me to figure out how to date a girl: what one did, where one went, and what she might desire. Those are the inevitable unknowns of adolescence, particularly for an isolated and somewhat neurotic farm boy. Moreover, I felt like I had no one to ask. Obviously I could not ask my parents—or more accurately, I was too embarrassed to ask them or show my vulnerability and ignorance by asking some other adolescent! Naiveté is inherent to childhood and early adolescence. It is forgivable then.

There is little excuse for it thereafter, particularly today. There are people everywhere who are open and willing to discuss such things, seriously or scandalously. My 11-year-old son is more aware and self-confident in these things than I was at 20. Moreover, it is his experience that he can talk with me about anything at all, that the Internet is totally accessible to him on his own laptop, and that there are a number of trusted adults around who are happy to listen to him and give him wholesome and, when appropriate, humorous guidance and reassurance.

I am surprised, but reassured, with the number of adults who seek out counselors like me to address their own naiveté about the matters of life and love. Such resources are readily available everywhere in the American world today. Moreover, pastors in general are open to and trained for assisting their parishioners with such private and intimate issues as must be thought through and sorted out, so to speak, if we are to grow healthier, happier, and more mature, spiritually and sexually. All of us need help sometimes, and some of us need help most of the time, coaching our lives along to optimal enjoyment. It is a good thing that in our culture today people are generally much more open to seeking help when they need it than they were a half century ago. We have accomplished some real gains in our experience of growth and relationality.

Unfortunately, there is nonetheless a considerable percentage of the human community that still falls into the pattern of what Lowen calls the sexually sophisticated but immature persons. He has great concern for their suffering and ineffectiveness in relationship, particularly sexually and with specific regard to orgasm. They remain consistently incapable of orgasm as spiritual experience—orgasm as the total connection with a lover in the experience of the pouring out of one's body, mind, and soul into that other person. The sexually sophisticated person, as we have said, knows everything that one can reasonably know about the form, technique, method, and psychology of lovemaking. However, his or her participation in making love remains on the level of stage performance rather than investing of one's self in another person.

Techniques of performance in making love to the point of orgasm can be learned from sources, but mere performance is the superficial preoccupation with acts of behavior that focus on themselves and the skill and art of the person performing. They are inherently narcissistic, directed toward one's self. This kind of lovemaking is about display, comparison, critique, and looking good. It has been correctly compared to table manners. If you are so preoccupied with your table manners that you cannot concentrate on the quality of the meal and the delights of its presentation or the aesthetics of the table setting and the room, you will fail to savor the flavor of the gourmet meal. You will be standing outside of the experience of the meal rather than enthusiastically participating in it with gusto.

The sexually sophisticated person stands outside of the process of his or her lovemaking, observing the quality of the performance rather than enthusiastically participating in it with invested vigor. Such a person cannot cast aside the self-centeredness of the lovemaking process and so is not able to abandon himself or herself to the experience of sexual play. This makes it impossible to achieve the transcendence of self necessary for full investment in the lover. When style of an experience becomes everything, content becomes nothing. That is true whether one is giving an important speech, performing an operation, or making love. It is designed to *impress* oneself or another person rather than *express* deep inner meanings.

It is our deep feelings, the language of the soul, that gives love and orgasm their meaning and validity. If my ego or my self-satisfaction is more important than the cherishing my lover feels from me and the fullness I give her body, mind, and spirit in my lovemaking, I may be sexually sophisticated, but I am not a real lover. Orgasm will be empty and not a spiritual experience for me or for her. And, of course, the same is true the other way around as well.

There are a number of performance issues that tend to arise today in the minds and sex-related behavior of what we are referring to as sexually sophisticated persons. Mainly those issues have to do with whether the sexually sophisticated person is successful in being able to achieve orgasm or bring his or her partner to orgasm.

Many men in this sophisticated age are sexual performers. Their sexual behavior has a compulsive element that is based upon their need to impress themselves and others with their sexual prowess. They are fixated upon their masculine egos, the symbol of which is the erect phallus. Where formerly such behavior belonged to the few (Casanova is a prime example), it now characterizes the sexual attitude of the many. So long as the compulsion exists, the sexual act will be a performance from which the risk of failure is never absent. When the compulsion is reduced or eliminated in the course of . . . therapy, the true feelings of the individual emerge.

What I have said about a man is equally applicable to a woman in her fear of sexual inadequacy, namely that she will not have an orgasm. Whether . . . a woman has an orgasm is no valid criterion of her adequacy . . . as a female. What kind of status symbol is orgastic potency in a woman or in a man, for that matter? . . . If she fails to achieve a climax . . . this may be owing to a variety of conditions over which she has no conscious control.[6]

Anxiety can cause this failure, as can guilt about sex, hostility toward the partner, disgust with sex partners in general, a sense of the sexual impotency of the lover, fear of penetration, feelings of sexual inadequacy, fear of pregnancy, or simply low self-esteem. If performance is everything for a woman or a man, she or he is likely to fail because performance anxiety will tend to ground out the energy needed for climax and for orgasm as pouring one's self out for one's lover. Coming away from such empty lovemaking and ungratifying orgasm leaves one feeling like all the little problems of life are enormously large ones. Sexual sophistication, as a lifestyle, must be eliminated if we expect to achieve sexual maturity and naturalness in our relationships. This, in turn, is necessary if we are to enjoy orgasm as spiritual experience.

In his important book *The Art of Loving*, Erich Fromm declared that "the answer to the problem of human existence 'lies in the achievement of interpersonal union, of fusion with another person, in *love*.'"[7] This uninhibited desire of union and communion with the object of our love is the central characteristic of the sexually mature personality, and it flows naturally to orgasm as spiritual experience. We long for closeness, indeed, enmeshment in body, mind, and spirit. In this longing, desire is the propellant, and what we desire, we love—in persons and things. "We desire to be close to those we love, and we love those toward whom we feel this desire." We wish to climax in the orgasmic experience of investing ourselves totally in our beloved.

The natural desires and wishes of love for arousal and orgasm have strong physical and spiritual dimensions. We naturally speak of love coming from the heart. If there is some reason that it is not from the heart, we do not think it is real; we do not trust it. Indeed, we fear such false pretensions. The heart is symbolically the center of our selves. We might say that the fact that true love must come from the heart is the heart of the matter. We use that word—heart—in so many different ways to refer to those values and experiences that are of central importance to us.

How often have you heard someone say, "You have touched my heart"? Spontaneously we know that it means you have expressed tender love to that person and incited love toward you in return. People will say, "He has a heart full of love" or "She has a heart for that work." We mean that such a person readily expresses love. We associate love with the organ, the heart, and we symbolize it rather crudely by drawing hearts on cards we send to express love. Symbolically, we learn early in life that the heart stands for true love.

The heart is the blood pump for our entire organism. It keeps our body, mind, and spirit going. This is not unrelated to the fact that when we are in a heartfelt communion with another person, and we desire real union with that person, the arousal we start to feel is generated by or incites an increase of the heart's work, pumping blood throughout our bodies. In this process the more we are aroused, the more blood is pumped into our erogenous zones. Progressively our genitals are engorged with blood, intensifying our desire, need, and readiness for sexual contact. The engorging blood causes our genitals to become literally hot. The male penis, engorged, achieves sturdy erection, prepared for penetration. The female vagina, clitoris, and mound of Venus, as they become engorged, feel an intense sensation of fullness, lubrication, and longing readiness for penetration. Surely it is literally important that one's heart is in it.

For sexually mature lovers, the resulting connection, communion, and union of the two highly charged erogenous zones, in penetration, pulsation, and gratification, inspires orgasm to become the healthy outpouring of an ecstasy that can properly be called spiritual. The meaning that flows from it can fill both lovers with a sense of the transcendent goodness of life. When lovemaking is not a performance for one's own ego, but an investing of self in one's lover, that wonderful sexual sensation makes all the big problems of life seem like little ones.

The ecstasy that makes big problems seem like little ones as we go along the roadway of life is surely a thing devoutly to be wished. It is interesting as well as important that we use this lovely word, *ecstasy*, to refer to both orgasm and mystical religious experiences. In ancient times, ecstasy was thought to be a special experience that God gave to special people in experiences of revelation and prophecy. When we use the term to refer to orgasm, we are not so far from that ancient idea as we might think. In one sense, everything I have been saying so far in this volume can be summarized in the simple notion that in orgasm as spiritual experience, we gain a fullness of gratification, meaning, and illumination.

In pouring ourselves out for our lover in healthy orgasm, we learn so much about our lover and ourselves that we would be truthful in calling it a season of revelation. We could surely refer to it as a transcendent illumination or revelation in the sense that it gives us a new level of awareness of ourselves and of life, which reaches heights beyond what we thought life to be before true love and the spirituality of fulfilling orgasm. It is not an accident that the biblical term for wholesome and mature sexual intercourse is "to know" the lover. It literally means to have the lover's inner and outer self revealed to us in the experience of pouring ourselves out into our lovers. The Bible refers to this "knowing" as so important and so enmeshing, as noted in a previous chapter, that it refers to the result as the experience of becoming one flesh; one body, mind, and spirit; one acting agent made up of the two persons.

Robert A. Johnson, in *Ecstasy, Understanding the Psychology of Joy*, implies distinctions similar to those we have teased out of Lowen's work regarding sexually sophisticated and sexually mature persons. Johnson launches his work with the following lament:

> It is the great tragedy of contemporary Western society that we have virtually lost the ability to experience the transformative power of ecstasy and joy. This loss affects every aspect of our lives. We seek ecstasy everywhere, and for a moment we may think we have found it. But, on a very deep level, we remain unfulfilled . . . We are looking for an exultation of the spirit; but instead of fulfillment we get a short-lived physical thrill that can never satisfy the chronic, gnawing emptiness with which we are beset. To fill this emptiness, we need to reconnect with the capacity for ecstasy that lies dormant within us. Our first step is to try to understand the nature of ecstasy.[8]

Johnson appropriately treats human ecstasy in religious mysticism and sexual orgasm as the same kind of human experience. Both transport us to transcendent levels of insight, illumination, meaning, and delight. Both reveal to us the true meaning of love, the true nature of our lovers, and the true gratification of a fulfilled life and tranquil joy. Both give us a memory to cherish, a present experience to savor, and a future expectation of the ecstasy to anticipate. Both create an aura of the goodness and meaningfulness of life on an entirely new plane of existence.

Johnson emphasizes that the degree to which we achieve the meaningful level of ecstasy for which we have the potential depends on the quality of the vision with which we live. If we look at life through its rectum, we will see only what the colon contains. There are a lot of people who have this crappy vision of life. They get from life what they envision. If, however, we embrace such values and views as afford us a positive and optimistic experience and expectation of life and love, we shall find that kind of joy as we make our way along. That is the difference between the trivial experience of the sexual sophisticate and the deep gratification of the mature lover. It has to do with one's belief system, our vision of the way the world is wired and of what we can expect from love and from life.

Such a belief system has to do with the story that we tell ourselves regarding how we understand and feel about the world, life, love, time, and eternity. That story is our master story, and into it we fit all the small stories of everyday experience that we have in life and love. I say we fit our little stories into this master story because it is our way of understanding and interpreting all the lesser events that occur to us as we go along. We build a master story, and that is our personal myth. I do not mean myth as a fairy tale or legend. I mean it as the truth that we hold to and believe is the correct understanding and interpretation of things.

Our personal myth or master story determines what we think of ourselves and what we expect from others and our relationship with others. Consequently, what we believe about life and love determines how we end up seeing the events and persons that make up our lives and loves. If we are egotistically preoccupied with mere performance and style in relationships, to demonstrate our superiority and prowess, that outlook will shape what we see, experience, and achieve in life and love. If we are mature personalities with a balanced and realistic view of ourselves, others, and our interaction, it is that healthy mythic vision of things that will determine what we experience in life and love.

Fortunately, we are able to test our master stories regularly in comparison with other people's master stories. We are able to include in our mythic vision the things people have learned about life and love in the past and have channeled down to us through our ancestors or our community and culture. Unfortunately, we live in a cultural moment when the mythic vision of our society—the master story of our social values—is in many ways antipathetic to, and works against, the enhancement of our own personal visions of reality. Many forms of counterproductive fantasy and triviality promote a materialistic standard for life and happiness. Experience of the spiritual quality and value of life and love seems downgraded, to say the least.

Johnson thinks that if we are to reconnect with the real ecstatic joy of life, we need to realign our values and hopes—our master story or mythic vision—with those qualities that can produce ecstasy in our spirituality and our sexuality. The loss of sexual and spiritual ecstasy has left a void in Western society. If we look for ecstasy in rational precision, material luxury, or powerful control of things, we shall not find it. It can be found only in relationship that has moved far beyond the rational, material, or volitional. Love is not rational, material, or an act of the will, and it is the only kind of relationship that can provide us ecstasy.

Paul Ricoeur, James B. Nelson, and many others saw the sexual revolution of the 1960s and 1970s as a time when ecstasy was torpedoed by the radical shearing off of spirituality from sexuality. Spirituality was relegated to the transcendent, and sexuality was trivialized as a mere practical earthy act of self-gratification. They now think we are moving into a new era when there is a longing in our culture to restore the union between the sexual and spiritual aspects of human experience. This is a time, they feel, when a few wise and authentic personalities here and there are restoring the connection between the transcendent and the mundane, between the heavenly and the earthy, between spirituality and the daily aspects of human life and love.

Perhaps that is true. Perhaps the unconscious motives for the preparation of this book, on the part of the author, and the publisher who suggested it, reflect this very process happening in this very instant. If you will pardon my use of the expression in this erotic context, I think "the proof of the pudding is in the eating." That is, whether we are in the process of a new and more wholesome movement in society that will enhance the growth of sexually mature personalities remains to be seen. If we are moving toward a time when orgasm can be an authentic spiritual experience for most human beings, I shall be very gratified, and humanity will be greatly healed in an enormous number of ways.

What can be said about this optimistic prospect is that we used to talk about spirituality or religion and sex, as though they were two different, remote, and opposing aspects of human existence. Now we talk about the spirituality *of* sex. We used to see books written about the theology of human sexuality; now we see titles such as *Sexual Theologies*. Whereas we used to hear a lot about sexuality being incidental or detrimental to the experience of God, now we think of sexuality as intrinsic to the human experience of our relationship with God. In my former work, *Sex in the Bible, A New Consideration*, I spilled a considerable amount of ink on discussing the notion of God's own sexuality.

Johnson points out that formerly we understood sexual sin as a matter of wrong sexual acts, and now we are talking about sexual sin more and more as any form of alienation from or repression of our God-designed and intended sexuality. Whereas we once spoke of salvation as though it was anti-sexual, now we use such language as "sexual salvation." Instead of seeing the church as an asexual community and ministers as asexual performers, we now think of the believing community as, among other things, a sexual community and pastors as sexual human beings. Issues of healthy sexuality have moved from the secretive private world to the public arena.[9]

These sound like major shifts—and wholesome ones. They represent a cultural and social revolution in sexuality and spirituality. They are surely remarkable gains for us to celebrate. A space is being created in our lives for us to deal openly with the issues of sexual and spiritual unity and wholeness. In this new freedom of thought and feeling, we shall achieve only what we can wholesomely envision. Whether we use this new psycho-spiritual opportunity in our world to become more mature lovers who can discover the full meaning of the spirituality of sex and orgasm will depend on the quality of our belief system. What do we really think about how the world is wired? What do we really believe about how authentic sexuality was designed by God to be? What can we imagine in our own quest for love?

If we envision mere sexual gymnastics, that is all we will get. If our master story is decked with the kind of values that impel us to reach out for transcendent experience in our relationship with God and with other lovers, we shall discover what God intended for us from the beginning. If we can believe that it is possible to really let go in our gift of ourselves to our lover, we shall find the revelation of truly "knowing" that person and his or her fulfillment, as well as our own. If we can abandon ourselves to the ecstatic release and freedom of investing completely in a lover, we shall be on the sure track of orgasm as spiritual experience. Pouring one's self out for the beloved in the ecstasy of orgasm is the ultimate achievement of the spirituality of sex.

> We touch, caress
> For kind response,
> So life is full
> And love is urgent.
>
> Crescendo starts
> Connection builds
> Communion leads
> To union's gasp
>
> Then with a leap
> Transcendence reigns
> We empty self
> To fill the loved
>
> That's not the end:
> A new beginning
> Of life and love
> And transformed selves

CHAPTER 8

TENDERNESS: THE CONTINUED CHERISHING

Some people have sex, roll over, and smoke a cigarette. Some just fall asleep. They are not lovers. They are narcissistic, self-gratifying gymnasts. As I have pointed out repeatedly, sex is not just the mechanics and gymnastics. It is making love, or it is subhuman and ungratifying for both lovers because it has nothing of the spiritual dimension of union and communion in it. It is mere physical self-gratification and in no sense a process of being really present to the beloved or of truly making love. Some people like just the mechanics. OK! But then life, love, and relationship remain superficial and trivial. Of course, that is all some people want out of life.

Alden, 26 years of age, was referred to my office by his very worried father. Immediately after leaving high school, Alden had fallen in love with a woman five years older than he. The woman, Meredith, had three small children and was still married, though abandoned by her husband. Alden courted her vigorously and seemed intensely delighted with the relationship, though his wealthy upper middle-class family of impeccable reputation viewed her to be a woman of ill-repute. She had been in and out of many legal entanglements and had been imprisoned for a time, having been convicted of a felony or two. Alden had always been a responsible worker and had a good steady job, but Meredith did not work, lived on welfare, and had spent a number of years being quite promiscuous.

Upon striking up a relationship with Alden, she seemed to set her life on a new and much more constructive course. Alden moved in with her, and she eventually became pregnant with his child. He really enjoyed his relationship with her, loved the experience of having a family, and set himself to a permanent life with Meredith and marriage. However, she refused to divorce her first husband, despite the fact that he failed to pay any child support. She feared if she raised the issue, he would seek custody of the children, what with her legal and sexual history. This impasse eventually led to Alden's departure from that little "family circle." He paid her child support for his son and retained visitation rights with him. Alden also had established a wholesome fatherly relationship with the other three children and so continued to cherish and nurture them, together with his son, whenever he had a chance to see them.

A year or so after his departure from that family circle, Alden met and courted a sophisticated, hard-working, moderately attractive female attorney his age, named Angelina. After a year or so of wooing each other, they were in love and planned their marriage. Alden's parents were appropriately pleased with this new turn of events and with the remarkably more attractive and admirable woman Alden had chosen. Alden liked the unusual amount of affirmation this brought him from his parents. The linkages with the family seemed to deepen greatly as time went on. Angelina was adopted as part of his family in a genuinely intimate way.

She brought a number of virtues to the relationship with Alden that his parents especially admired. She earned a good salary and managed money wisely. She was an imaginative mother to Alden's son. She took over the finances of the couple and did well, though Alden noticed that in the process she kept him on a very short rope. That was probably a stroke of wisdom on her part. However, this capacity for careful control began to show up in her management of their social life and friendships as well. She could order things in a systematic way and run a good show. This mystified Alden because it contrasted with her slovenly management of their new home. He worked hard to give it order and beauty. This seemed to mean nothing to her, and her presence in the home always left it looking like it had been hit by a tornado.

In less than a year of marriage, Alden became troubled by Angelina's apparently complete lack of interest in working with him to create in their new house an orderly, clean, and aesthetic space. It was not so much that she was preoccupied with work or could not find the time. Her corporate job was strictly a nine to five routine, and she had a lot of free time. However, she was obsessed with jogging and running marathons. They had enough money so that she had the discretionary cash to go almost anywhere in the country, at the drop of a hat, to run in a marathon for this cause or that, by one excuse or another. Consequently, she was perpetually in training, running long distances every evening after work. Alden could not say much about the financial cost, given that she earned twice as much as he did. However, he got to the point that he could not bear to invite his meticulous parents to their home.

She was an attractive woman, obviously in good shape and full of vim, vigor, and vitality, and all that exercise did not diminish her availability for sex. However, her lovemaking was a "slam, bam, thank you, man" sort of thing. Alden never felt that Angelina really connected with him in their sexual play. It seemed to him to be rather mechanical as time when on, and he noticed that if he did not initiate it, a month could go by, and she would not seem to notice the absence of sexually intimate times. Indeed, when they did make love, it seemed to him like she was not even there.

This represented a radical contrast to Meredith, who had made love like she was investing her whole self in it every time, without reservation, and as if there were no tomorrow! Being a sensitive and tender type of personality, Alden longed for a relationship with Angelina in which she seemed to really want and need him and his cherishing love. She never gave evidence of feeling that way or having that kind of interest or nature. No matter what he tried to do to really please her, it was always received with a matter-of-fact response. He was able to finally put the right word on it in therapy. He was looking for *sustained tenderness*. She was looking for a quick orgasm and a five-mile run.

The sex itself was good enough, he thought, but there was no significant foreplay in their lives together and, worst of all, no sustained tenderness after the climax of love. She simply did not seem to need that tenderness, and Alden began to fear that she was not capable of expressing that. She did not seem to know there was such a thing. It turned out that he was correct. She was incapable of investing herself in any other person, in any of her friendships, work relationships, or nuclear family. Everything was at arm's length. She was sexually sophisticated, good at the mechanics, and proud of her performance but incapable of pouring herself out for and into another person in any setting. She was a delightfully achieving professional lady, but the only relationship she could establish was the breathless exchange of brief phrases between breaths, while jogging with another runner.

Angelina was all about the ego gratification of performance: performance at work, performance in marathons, and performance at sex. She seemed preoccupied with proving to herself how great she was, except as a homemaker, a space in life that nobody observed. That space was irrelevant to her because it could not be made into a stage for performance; she did not care to take the time to invite others to her home to entertain them. She did not invest in others in that way. She was too busy with personal ego-gratification. People like that are pathological, and they should be called on it. They are afraid of real relationship, or they do not believe there is such a thing, or they cannot conceive of it, or they do not believe that they can achieve it. Of course, truly making love is much more profound than such superficiality. It is a playful process that begins long before the sexual mechanics and continues in *shared tenderness* long after gratifying orgasm. The natural tenderness of

real lovemaking normally follows the psychospiritual experience of caressing, arousal, union, and orgasm. It is a matter of nurturing one's lover with
tenderness for as long as time and duty permit.

For most women and many fortunate men, the foreplay of psychospiritual
presence to one another that makes sexual union so gratifying is the many
tender moments that can be offered all along the way of daily life. Life is foreplay, and making love is the frequent bursts of profound union of body, soul,
and spirit that are spontaneously produced in joyful relationship when life
is lived as foreplay. Surely we have nailed these realities down well enough
already in this book.

It will not take the average reader long, at this point, to identify the likely
reason Alden's father referred him for therapy. Alden was increasingly disillusioned with his marriage to Angelina. He loved his little son and visited
him frequently each week. Meredith encouraged him to visit any time he
wished to and could do so. She urged him to stay with his boy for as long as
he wanted to and had time for it. His delight with the four children and with
the openness and warmth of Meredith soon led them both into a restoration
of their former intimacy. Alden filed for divorce, and everybody was stunned.
How could he trade off such a beautiful and accomplished professional lady
for this unattractive felon and formerly disreputable woman of the streets?
Easy! *Sustained and sustaining tenderness!* The *spirituality* of sex!

The tenderness that precedes and follows profound sexual union is what
makes a relationship spiritual rather than merely a series of libidinous spasms
and releases. Sustained and sustaining tenderness is the continuation of the
cherishing investment of my self in my lover that makes sexual play into
authentic lovemaking. That tenderness is a continuation of the pouring of
myself out in love for and into my lover.

Jerry drove a new, red sports car of very expensive vintage. He was a
young engineer with a good corporate job, so he had a right to believe that
his future was secure and that he could afford to indulge himself in such
a symbol of prowess and phallic style. He was also very pleased with how
muscular he was getting from pumping iron three days a week at the Esquire
Club. He attracted an interesting crowd of colleagues his age and, of course,
was much sought after by the most attractive women at work and at the club.
He could be seen any weekend with a truly lovely and attentive blond model
on his arm or in his car; and he wore them well, like a badge of superior
achievement. Most of his colleagues agreed and admired him, not without
some jealousy.

What always mystified me, however, and what eventually seemed to get
the attention of the group with whom he spent much of his time was the fact
that one almost never saw him with the same woman twice, or at least not
for a more sustained time than a month or two. This was strange because he
seemed like a nice, playful guy with enough money to treat a woman in a way

that would keep her interested as long as he was interested. Eventually, a woman whom he had courted for a somewhat longer time than seemed usual for him appeared in my office in great distress. She had been disposed of by him, rather peremptorily, upon telling him after six months of courtship and intimacy that he seemed more preoccupied with himself than really interested in her. It had not been her intent to criticize him but to discuss some fine-tuning in their relationship.

She had been feeling for some months that their relationship and sexual play were mostly about his display of himself and less about their building any kind of mutuality. She genuinely loved many things about him, felt a real devotion to him, and enjoyed being kind, tender, and caring toward him. He had always seemed to her to soak up all the tender loving care she could give him and to enjoy it immensely. However, she often felt that he was much better at receiving it than responding with similar emotion. He tended instead to move from their moments of her tenderness into some form of playful activity in the world of sports or partying, as though he thought that would be a gratifying reward for her. She had finally come to the point of realizing that such activities were carefully crafted distractions that helped him avoid the need to pour himself into intimate sharing with her.

She decided to raise the matter in discussion with him when she noticed that this was not just a pattern of behavior with her but that he controlled all his relationships in this way. He allowed people to wash him with their love or fawning, but he gave nothing in return except the mechanics of carefully managed entertainments. Life was not about relationship for him. It was about consuming whatever he could possess for his gratification, with nothing returned in the form of connection, communion, or union. She realized that their sexual play was a display of his prowess and muscular body, a release of his libidinal arousal, and a process of sucking all the vitality out of his lover. She asked herself, "What is wrong with this picture?" Her answer: "The absence of *sustained and sustaining tenderness.*"

The hotshot who had thrown her away was fun, in many ways a nice guy, and sometimes generous, but he was consummately incapable of tenderness toward her or anyone. His narcissism was so pervasive in his personality that he was inherently incapable of any behavior except that which called attention to his large muscles, sporty car, rakish popularity, phallic notoriety, and sexual prowess. Such people can be genuinely entertaining, high achieving, aesthetically colorful, and the life of the party.

Unfortunately, they cannot build relationships. They illegitimately wear their clothes, cars, style, and women in the opposite way from the manner in which a soldier legitimately wears his Meritorious Service Medal, Legions of Merit, or Congressional Medal of Honor. The stud has claimed everything and earned nothing, whereas the soldier has earned everything and claimed nothing. The warrior is capable of sustained tenderness; the stud is limited to puffing his ego. There is no room there for the tender love required in cherishing a lover.

Even the most imaginative and tender-hearted male has a tough enough time figuring out just exactly how a woman feels about tenderness and love and what she needs in order to experience sustained and sustaining tenderness. Therefore, how can we expect a narcissistic and self-idolizing man to become a truly wise lover? It is impossible. I do not mean that there is something wrong with women that makes them hard to figure out. I mean that it is difficult for men to discern what seems to women like sustained and sustaining tenderness. Women seem to have more intuition about what that dimension of relationship takes and can usually figure out what men need and desire in their hunger for gentleness and tenderness. The average healthy woman seems to discern that automatically from childhood onward. That is directly related to the fact that most men spend most of their time in their left brain: linear logic, analysis, and bottom-line thinking. Women spend most of their time in their right brain: beauty, emotion, color, texture, and relationality.

One of the most interesting things at play in this instance is the difference in the way most men and most women savor the flavor of relationship, even wholesome, healthy, full-orbed, and authentic love relationship. Taking the model of life as foreplay, and all the small tender moments along the way in any given week or day as the heightening of that intensity of lovemaking, it is in the end the case that women are *more* oriented on the process and men are *more* oriented on the climax. That is the way God has wired us. There are emotional, psychological, intellectual, and biological reasons for this interesting difference. It is necessary to consider them carefully if we care about tenderness as the continued cherishing of true love.

Because 70 percent of the men in the world are left-brain dominant, and the other 30 percent are high on both left- and right-brain scales, men are generally good at fixing faucets, making the garage door work, putting the do-it-yourself cabinet together, acquiring math skills, constructing corporations, running factories, and making sure the bottom line comes out to their advantage. They are interested in the process, in each case, but their primary concern is the finished project, the bottom line, the solution.

Seventy percent of the women in the world are right-brain dominant, and the other 30 percent are high on both right- and left-brain scales. That is why most women are better than most men at tenderly caring for babies, teaching small children, nurturing injured and needy persons, building relationships, finding beauty in simple and intimate things, and creating life-styles of aesthetic idealism and warmth. They are interested in the final outcome, in each case, but their primary concern is the process of how things feel and unfold along the way. Men look for the end product, women savor the flavor of the developing process.

Of course, it must be said that many men are nurturing and appreciative of the development process of life and relationship, and many women are very instrumental and can fix faucets and make that damn toilet stop running forever, but the differences of preference and orientation persist, nonetheless. The point here is that these differences carry over into our relationships of spirituality and sexuality. Healthy and mature men, for example, genuinely desire, think about, and try to contribute to life as foreplay, from morning to night and day after day. They really want and like to create an ongoing relationship of cherishing and delightful emotional and erotic playfulness with their wives, friends, or lovers. They are genuinely pleased when this life of foreplay regularly unfolds in seasons of overt sexual arousal, communion, and union.

In the end, however, for every man the real intimate achievement is experienced in the climax. That is when he really feels the full thrust of his pouring himself out for his lover. The ultimately gratifying and intimate event is orgasm. That is the bottom line! That is the climax of the utter spirituality of sexuality in a deep relationship. For a man, the sustained and sustaining tenderness that can follow orgasm is a leftover of emotion from the energy of the orgasm. He may continue to feel that for minutes, hours, or days, depending on his personality and the congeniality of his lover's attentiveness and response. But orgasm is the bottom line.

For women this entire experience is somewhat different. Healthy and mature women, of course, also genuinely desire, think about, and try to contribute to life as foreplay, from morning to night and day after day. For most wholesome, healthy women, however, this process is much more spontaneous, natural, and intuitive than it is for men. They too really need and desire to create a free-flowing relationship of cherishing emotion and erotic playfulness with their husbands, friends, or lovers. They are quite clear on the expectation that whenever they wish to entice their lover to it, this life of foreplay will readily unfold into times of overt sexual arousal, communion, and union.

The interesting thing about this experience for women, however, is that the process is as important as the climax. Many of my female patients, parishioners, and friends tell me that the process is quite a bit more important to them than the outcome in orgasm. My most trusted confidant on these matters said to me recently,

> Orgasm is fine—I would even say it is wonderful—but what really counts for me is the tenderness of the hours and days leading up to it, the intensity of the arousal when we are free to actually make love, the touching all over my body, and then the wonderful warmth and tranquility in the hours after climax. That is what counts for me. I feel infinitely gentle, and so does my husband. I can sense it. I feel then like God is in his heaven, and all is right with the world; and whatever the problems are in the whole world, they will be healed.

Nearly half a century ago, Ashley Montague wrote a most amazing book that he called, simply, *Touching*.[1] In it he explains why my friend feels so completely loved when her lover "touches her all over her body." *Touching* is a book about the importance of the human skin. The skin is the largest organ of our bodies, and until very recently, it has been the most neglected, in both popular knowledge and scientific investigation. Montague points out that in all relationship issues, the skin is a crucial functioning factor. Touch is so important to us. He says the skin has a mind of its own. It tells us which is a kind relationship and which a harsh one. It signals when we are in danger and when we are loved.

> The skin, like a cloak, covers us all over, the oldest and most sensitive of our organs, our first medium of communication, and our most efficient of protectors. Perhaps, next to the brain, the skin is the most important of all our organ systems. The sense most closely associated with the skin, the sense of touch, "the mother of the senses," is the earliest to develop in the human embryo. When the embryo is less than an inch long from crown to rump, and less than eight weeks old, light stroking of the upper lip or wings of the nose will cause bending of the neck and trunk away from the source of stimulation. At this stage in its development the embryo has neither eyes nor ears. Yet its skin is already highly developed.[2]

I have realized for a long time that there is a thing called skin hunger. When I was a young army chaplain, stationed at Fort Riley with the First Infantry Division, my supervisor, Chaplain (MAJ) John Betzold, told me one morning to go to the Post Hospital to visit a 92-year-old lady, the military dependent and mother of one of our master sergeants. I was an inexperienced 23-year-old clergyman, and I wondered what I had to talk about with, or offer to, a 92-year-old woman. Betzold said, "Just remember that inside that elderly lady is a young, sexy, 18-year-old girl. Find that girl and give her some warmth and encouragement. Hold her hand and touch her shoulder."

I did just that, and the patient's response was glowing and grateful. I did not need to figure out what to talk about. She had lots to talk about, and we had a mutually enjoyable visit. I visited her regularly while she remained in the hospital and after she returned to quarters and recuperated. A spontaneous friendship sprang up between us because I had found the real person inside that withered elderly lady. All it really took was a grasp of her hand and a touch on her shoulder. I have realized ever since that few people realize, and it is too easily overlooked, how little elderly people get touched. Now I am an old man, and I can tell you that nobody ever touches old men. If I want or need to be touched, I must pay for a massage. I realize now that the elderly patient at Fort Riley had a strong sense of skin hunger, just as I do today. We need to be touched tenderly and often. Everyone does.

In 1965 I attended the Cranbrook Institute for Advanced Pastoral Studies, conducted by the famed Dr. Ruel Howe. The seminar lasted two weeks and was a profound experience of deep probing into the nature and impact of various pastoral care and counseling strategies. I learned a great deal from that experience and enjoyed the fellowship and discussion with the 24 other participants. We dealt with very intimate matters regarding ourselves and our ministries to specific needy people in our parishes. During the last two days of the seminar, as one would expect, we began the process of summing up and debriefing. The leader suggested a special exercise to assist in that. He urged each of us to write a haiku to capture the meaning of our seminar experience.

A haiku, of course, is a most cryptic form of verbal statement. It is a kind of a Japanese poem. It has a very precise and inflexible form. Its structure is designed in three lines. The first is five syllables or beats, the second seven, and the third five again. I was very surprised with what came to my mind after struggling for half a day or so with the assignment. To this day I am quite pleased with my haiku:

What the hell is hell,
If not the real painfulness
Of no hand to touch?

This experience reinforced my developing awareness of how intense our need for tender touch is. Nothing conveys to us so directly the sustained and sustaining cherishing for which our whole beings hunger, all the way through, from our skin to our psyches and back out again. Two lovers fondly touching, caressing, and fondling each other in the crescendo of sexual arousal, sexual-spiritual communion, and orgasmic union; and then holding each other tenderly, skin to skin, after the climax of lovemaking, feel like they have died and gone to heaven. Rosetti said it best in "The Kiss."

I was a child beneath her touch,—a man
When breast to breast we clung, even I and she,—
A spirit when her spirit looked through me,—
A god when all our life-breath met to fan
Our life-blood, till love's emulous ardours ran,
Fire within fire, desire in deity.[3]

When lovemaking turns out to be mechanical, and no tenderness or sustained cherishing follows, it hurts like hell and is a wounding curse. This is true for both men and women, but women feel it even more deeply than men do. Just as orgasm for men is the ultimate experience, and for women the process is crucially important, so failed tenderness or lack of it leaves a greater wounding in women than in men. Men try to rationalize in the analytical left brain the hellish hurt when tenderness is lacking and try to get beyond it. It seems to me that women feel it stuck deeply in their right-brain emotionality, and it becomes a persisting cancer in their intuitive unconscious.

A large part of this interesting difference between men and women is biological. It is not a surprise that for men the moment of orgasm is a watershed event, given that men are basically capable of only one orgasm at a time and need to wait for an hour or so before they are "recharged," so to speak. Some men claim they can have multiple orgasms, and you can buy manuals that claim they will teach males how to have multiple orgasms, but that is bunk. If a man has what he is calling a multiple orgasm, it is simply a matter of his not having completed the original one, having distracted himself (probably by thinking about having multiple orgasms), and then needing to return to focus on his lover to complete that original orgasm.

On the other hand, women are biologically and psychologically capable of multiple orgasms. In fact, all healthy women are capable of almost an infinite number of orgasms, limited only by their physical endurance. When a woman tells you that her lover simply drives her crazy, she usually means that he stimulates her to such intense orgasms and to so many of them in succession that she nearly loses consciousness. That is a real possibility for any healthy woman. The literature is replete with reports of women who were so highly stimulated in making love that they experienced a repetition of orgasms that literally brought them to the point of fainting into unconsciousness. That is an ultimate achievement of the intense spasms of orgasms. Moreover, highly sensitive and erotically responsive women are able to orgasm at the mere touch of a lover to any of her erogenous zones. That kind of responsiveness is an enormous delight to her lover.

Some women, for example, in the intense process of making love with a truly tender lover, will have a large orgasm if he merely touches her underarm or lower back, or if he kisses her eyelid. A similar response will be aroused if he gently rolls one of her distended nipples between his fingers or flicks it with his tongue. Moreover, a kiss that expresses sustained tenderness and a deep love for her will bring the average woman to an intense orgasm. A deep French kiss, active and invasive, may produce multiple orgasms for most women.

Manual stimulation of her clitoris, or the outer and inner lips of her vagina, will make a woman orgasm brilliantly if it is in the context of sustained and sustaining tender lovemaking. Even manual contact with her cervix will stimulate the same response, and of course, penis penetration and intercourse usually causes a healthy and erotically responsive woman to orgasm repeatedly if she feels the kind of trust and tenderness for her lover that sets her free to pour herself completely out to him.

So these differences in the effects of tenderness in men and women must be understood if we are to cherish each other well and understand the responses we generate in doing so. If men were forced to choose between the process of lovemaking and orgasm, most would vote for orgasm. If women were compelled to decide between the two, almost all would opt for the *process* of making love. The reasons are strictly biological and physiological. Of course, if both men and women can have both, they will both choose the process *and* the orgasm, but for slightly different reasons and with slightly different emphases and priorities. After orgasm, most women want to nest, and most men feel empowered and able to fix all the faucets and conquer the world.

If you can understand this, you will love your man or woman all the more, and all the better. You will automatically want to explore and exploit the infinite possibilities of tender and healing touch in making love. Montague emphasized that "the greatest sense in our bodies is our touch sense . . . we feel, we love and hate, are touchy and are touched, through the touch corpuscles of our skin."[4] During the last half of the twentieth century, we learned a great deal about the healing power of touch. Everyone has heard of the experiment with monkeys in which those who were touched, handled, fondled, and manually fed tended to thrive nicely, whereas those who were isolated, never touched or fondled, and fed mechanically wasted away and died. What most of us do not remember is the experience of English and American infant foundlings in orphanages during the eighteen and nineteenth centuries. They tended to be "warehoused" and given little personal attention or touching and handling, and nearly 100 percent died.

The "Dr. Spock" of the late nineteenth century was Emmett Holt, Sr., professor of pediatrics at New York Polyclinic and Columbia University. He advocated the abolition of the cradle and urged that babies be left alone with little touching and handling; he recommended not picking up the baby when it cried, bottle feeding by the clock, and avoiding breastfeeding, cuddling, and "spoiling the child." Dr. Henry Dwight Chapin, a distinguished New York pediatrician realized how emotionally arid such a non-touching program was, lacking in nurture and relationship, and what a high mortality rate resulted from it.

He and his colleague, Fritz Talbot of Boston, developed the idea of "tender loving care." They were following on the experience that Dr. Talbot had seen in the Children's Clinic of Dusseldorf, whose director was Dr. Arthur Schlossmann. Talbot noted that the German clinic was efficiently run, that it was neat and clean, and that there was a somewhat higher ratio of attendants to children than was typical in England and America. Then he noted a fat old lady carrying around a very measly child. When he asked Dr. Schlossmann about it, the director replied, "Oh, that is Old Anna. When we have done everything we can medically for a baby, and it is still not doing well, we turn it over to Old Anna, and she is always successful."[5]

The fact that humans who are deprived of touch and nurture do not thrive, in infancy or adulthood, was given a diagnostic name already in the nineteenth century, taken from an ancient Greek word. It was called *marasmus*, which means "wasting away." However, it took us until after World War II to study thoroughly what caused it. It was discovered that babies in wealthy homes and in orphanages suffered from marasmus, and their mortality rate was higher than that of children in poor and less sanitary homes. The differential factor proved to be touch, handling, fondling, body contact, and close social connections.

As early as 1938, the Bellevue Hospital in New York introduced an emphasis on "mothering" in its pediatric wards. Their mortality rates for infants fell from 35 percent to 10 percent that year. Dr. Brennemann established the rule that all the babies must be picked up, fondled, played with, carried around, nurtured, cuddled, and mothered several times each day. Humans thrive under healing touch. When lovemaking is mediated with tender touch, and our skin hunger is gratified by sustained and sustaining cherishing after climax, we thrive. When that is not true for us, we are at risk.

Elderly people live 20 years longer when they are in a congenial intimate relationship than when they are single. Recently a woman physician at Harvard is reported to have determined by empirical experimentation that it is measurably therapeutic for a senior adult male to view for 10 minutes daily the breasts of a woman whose body conveys the aura of fertility and warmth. This procedure reduces blood pressure and heart risk by a significant measurable degree. I understand why that is true. If so, how much more healing is the tender touch of a lover then? It causes children to live and thrive, and it affects adults the same way.

Judith C. Lechman, commenting on sustained and sustaining tenderness in relationship, said that it is all about learning to give ourselves utterly to a relationship, without pride.[6] An eighteenth-century Quaker named John Woolman said in his own quaint manner that whoever in the world has a heart that expresses itself in perfect sincerity to its beloved, and in whom this has taken root and grows as a way of life together, has found the community of true love relationship, and that is a gift of God.[7]

I have noticed in myself, and in my close relationships with kind and loving women, that from childhood onward, I longed for that intimacy that made me feel like I had recovered my "other half," so to speak. My mother was ill a great deal when I was an infant and small child. My sister, just older than I, died when still small. That was a desperate loss for my parents. My next brother was born 17 months after me and so took my mother's attention from me, when she was well enough to attend at all. In those early years I was raised by two loving aunts. However, I think it was not because of those circumstances, but that it is universally human, that I felt from birth on, so far as I can remember, a very great loss and emptiness deep inside. I longed for my mother, of course, but at the appropriate time in late puberty, I began to realize a shift of that longing toward girlfriends.

I remember it as an extremely intense and irrepressible attraction. Initially I was not aware of the fact that it had sexual and genital dimensions. I just felt desperately in need of finding a friendship and connected relationship that took away my emptiness, that gave me back my other half, which I seemed to have lost on departure from the womb. This gnawing and drawing attraction grew and became more painful as I progressed through adolescence because I was too neurotic to figure out how to relate to girls and so never really had a girlfriend in a sustained relationship. Working my way through college and graduate school left me too busy to date much. When I really fell in love, I felt like I had finally become a whole person for the first time.

This is a fairly typical male odyssey, except that most adolescent boys and young men these days are less neurotic and more successful in dating, thus gaining more insight earlier about the nature and value of real relationship. Nonetheless, for males, the longing for a female friend, companion, and lover is the irrepressible need to regain our other half and become whole persons in a relationship of sustained and sustaining tenderness, love, union, and ecstasy. It prompts males, even robustly brusque and aggressive males, to be tender, gentle, and sustained in our cherishing toward the women we love and who we sense love us. We can hardly wait, through adolescence to young adulthood, to pour ourselves out for a true and durable lover.

Women have similar longings for fulfillment, of course. As we court and woo each other in our young lives of encounter and connection, that longing in females looks very much like it looks in males. The cherishing behavior looks like women are longing and looking for their completion as whole persons in a true and profoundly tender love relationship with their favorite man. Men are pleased to experience this, as women are pleased to note the longing and pursuit of men seeking after them. This process appropriately leads to connections that ultimately become genuine communion, union, marriage, and committed relationships. It is really a wonderful and delightful process, all in all, for women and men alike.

There is, however, one interesting glitch that often arises in this process. Children arrive on the scene and require a great deal of nurturing attention. In consequence, in most cases, the attention of the mother is shifted toward the child or children, if for no other reason than the need to nurse and nurture the children. However, it is too often the case that the shift never shifts back, so the mother's attention to the marriage relationship is never restored. In fact, it often proves to be the case that the wife in such marriages never really found her other half in her husband, but expressed intense tenderness and attention to her husband because *unconsciously* she sensed that as a way to get her womb hunger satisfied. Her unconscious inner longing was really for finding her completion, her wholeness as a person, in her children. Women find their other half in their progeny, the fruit of their wombs. That is the way God wired it.

There are two important implications of this reality. First, it illustrates another reason, among the many that one can cite, for husbands to share equally with their wives in the nurture and care of their children at all phases of the children's development. Second, both husbands and wives do well to be attentive to the damage that can be done to themselves, their relationship, and their children when the wife in the marriage wanders off emotionally, so to speak, into a world of preoccupation with *her* children and herself, at the expense of her husband and the marriage relationship.

My estimate is that this happens 90 percent of the time. Moreover, most children are born between the mother's age of 20 and 35. That means that when they are finally off to college, and the nest is empty, she is becoming menopausal or postmenopausal. The result is that she does not have a significant union with her husband any longer because she has grown accustomed to finding her wholeness in her children, who are now gone from the nest. So she has no interest and built-in channels of connection and communion with her husband anymore. She does not know what it would be like to be intimately connected and tenderly sharing with a man who is now 55 years old or more. She has had years of a practical friendship with him in his caring companionship, but virtually no deep union, for two decades. He is in many ways a stranger in *her* house.

Wife and husband do not know how to reconnect and are probably embarrassed with their distance and emotional isolation from each other, and she does not have any of the old urges for womb fulfillment left to drive her into intimacy and real connection with him again. So she hangs out with her girlfriends, seeks new forms of spirituality, changes her diet, vacations alone, and generally dives into a world he cannot share and is not invited to know and understand. What has gone wrong? She has gotten what she always needed, womb fulfillment, in bearing children. She has expended her tenderness and nurturing needs on her children. They have responded in ways that have filled her life with enormous gratification. She has decreased more and more the tenderness expressed to her husband and ignored or closed out the tenderness he has tried to show to her. Perhaps by that time he has understandably given up. The result is a sterile old age of loss and loneliness for both. They have lost out on what John Woolman called a great gift of God.

Of course, I have this dear woman friend who tells me that sex for her is enormously better after menopause than before. Now she has no anxiety about the possibility of pregnancy. There are no children in the next room whispering to each other in gleeful exasperation, "Oh God, they are doing it again!" There is more time for just tenderness and holding each other. The afterplay can be as nice as the foreplay. Life just seems so whole and complete finally.

The tenderness of continued cherishing is crucial to keeping alive in a marriage or any relationship of lovers that hunger to gently touch and be touched by one another. Real connection, meaningful communion, and authentic union between lovers in a sustained and sustaining relationship of love requires a harmony of their souls. This harmony needs to take a form that causes them to feed and fulfill the skin hunger they both feel if they are tending their relationship responsibly. It is physical touching that keeps the souls alive to each other. It is the skin that is the organ of such life-giving nurture. This epidermal caressing leads to the deeper expressions of their love.

The fact is that in no other kind of connection is the touching and caress of the skin so crucial as in love and the sexual play love engenders. Touch, caress, frequent stimulation of each other's skin, and tender loving care of each to the other produces spontaneous and authentic connection. From that follows arousal, excitement about each other, enthusiasm for one another, true sustaining tenderness, and orgasm. Those who neglect each other and this process seal their own doom. Those who care enough to make the appropriate effort and to take the inevitable risks of connecting or reconnecting build for themselves a real heaven on earth.

There it is
The gentle tender touch,
Sustained and sustaining nurture
For all life's grand experiment
And exciting undertakings
In love.

Here it is
The nest to nurture children,
The perpetual invitation,
Life in the aura of joy,
Hatching out an enriched future
Of love.

Where is it
Going to be tomorrow?
Can I care to keep love lively?
Can I count on you for that?
Are we just two cool friends: no warmth,
No love?

We could try
The simple tender touching
That we knew well so long ago.
And startle awake again
The kind and gentle tenderness.
True love.

CHAPTER 9

THE HEALING POWER OF SEXUALITY, SENSUALITY, AND SEXUAL PLAY

Life lived as foreplay, in which frequent occasions of making love can be counted on, heals us. Such love and life leave the lovers with a constant aura of tenderness until the next occasion for intimacy arises. The healing power of such sex and sensuousness braces and embraces the body, mind, and spirit of every human being lucky enough to have such cherishing relationship. As we have already noted, plenty of empirical data now demonstrates that people who live into advanced old age with a tender lover or kind caregiver tend to live as much as a couple decades longer than people who live alone. To live alone or in a cantankerous and uncherishing relationship is deadly!

Such longevity in tenderly cherished persons seems to be a result of the fact that living life sensually and sexually is healing. The evidence should not surprise us. People who feel profoundly cherished feel more completely whole. They also feel far less anxious, hopeless, or helpless. Moreover, sustained joyful intimacy enhances that sense of wholeness, in younger people as well as in the elderly. That is true whether the intimacy is intellectual, emotional, psychological, social, spiritual, or sexual. However, in persons who live life sensually and sexually, while also living in touch with their inner selves, this healing benefit seems to be greatly increased. Feeling a strong sense of wholeness in body, mind, and spirit strengthens one's immune system. That guards against all sorts of illness, including many forms of cancer. So sexuality and sensuality as a mode of life have profound healing power.

Interesting insights have come to us over the last half century from the many scientific studies that have been carried out and the numerous reports rendered on human need for sensuality and sexual experience. Anna Freud frequently suggested that sensuous stimulation had significant healing power already in the life of infants.[1]

> At the beginning of life being stroked, cuddled, and soothed by touch libidinizes the various parts of the child's body, helps to build up a healthy body image and body ego, and simultaneously promotes the development of object love by cementing the bond between child and mother. There is no doubt that, at this period the surface of the skin in its role as erotogenic zone fulfills a multiple function in the child's growth.[2]

Undoubtedly that is related to the healing power Old Anna possessed and exercised in Dr. Schlossmann's Children's Clinic in Dusseldorf, cited in the previous chapter. Anna Freud's strong recommendation that maternal sensual stimulation of infants and children empowers them for greater sensual and sexual comfort and normalcy as adolescents and adults cannot be overestimated and should surely not be underestimated.

Studies of rhesus monkeys, replicated by numerous scientists in a variety of settings over the last hundred years or so, indicated that motherless female monkeys who were not cuddled, held, fondled, and sensuously stimulated as infants and children did not have normal openness to sensual attraction and behavior as adult monkeys. They never showed normal female sexual posturing or response when in heat and in the presence of male monkeys. They eventually were impregnated simply because the males patiently persisted in their sexual pursuit. Adequate sensual mothering is necessary for appropriate development of healthy sensual and sexual life in adults.[3]

An early study by Professor Marc H. Hollender, of the University of Pennsylvania Department of Psychiatry, followed a number of women who presented with difficulties in developing and maintaining relationship. It turned out that their distress, in each case, related directly to their unfulfilled need to be held and cuddled. Body contact seems to be an intense and indispensable need in all human beings. This is related both to our universal skin hunger and to our irrepressible hunger for deep inner connection and union. So our outer shell, so to speak, and our inner heart both need the continual stimulation of sensuality and sexuality in order to sustain a sense of spiritual wholeness and health. That is, our entire selves, in order to be whole selves, are designed in such a way as to require constant or regular sensual and sexual stimulation so as to function wholesomely and have a thoroughgoing sense of spiritual health and well-being.

Adults react in surprising ways if they have been sensually and sexually deprived during their developmental years. Hollender found that some felt body contact as adults was so disagreeable and even repugnant that they were unable to sustain even a normal friendship. On the other hand, some who had been similarly deprived had an extreme, indeed virtually desperate, need for body contact, to the point of a nearly addictive compulsion. The consequence of this was development of a life of promiscuity. Our normal need for sensual body contact from infancy to old age, like our oral needs, are intense and tend to increase in times of stress. Oral needs can be fulfilled with normal eating and drinking, but our body-contact longings require the attention and sustained sensual stimulation by another person whom we can trust and care about at some level of connection.

Some of the women in Hollender's study used sex to attract males just to get them to hold and cuddle them. They were not necessarily seeking sexual intercourse, but just the sensual body contact. Some of the women asked friends outright to hold and caress them, making it clear that they were not asking for sex. Others asked openly for friends to give them both sensuous caressing and sexual play, as well as intercourse and orgasm. It is a very common experience in clinical work to have a patient say that he or she is in a relationship in which there is very little cherishing and only the mechanics of sex, without real union and communion. Such persons often insist that what they really miss is someone to hold them.

> [Some] women may entice men to sex relations when their real desire is to be held or cuddled. As one of these women put it, in describing her desire to be held, "It's a kind of an ache . . . It's not like an emotional longing for some person who isn't there; it's a physical feeling." . . . "In a way, I used sex to be held" . . . At best . . . the sexual experiences of these intensely unhappy people seem more an attempt to make some sort of human contact, however incomplete, than to achieve physical satisfaction.[4]

This is a more common complaint from women than from men. I have often speculated, however, and am now quite certain, that the difference is not one of need. Both have equal need for body contact. The difference between men and women arises from the fact that women are more willing to speak of their inner needs and emotional longings than are men. I am sure we can say the same of men as we have said of women in the preceding discussion. I frequently hear from a patient that she wonders whether her husbands really loves her because whenever she gives him any indication that she would like to be close to him, have him hold and caress her, and just kiss and be tender to her, he immediately gets sexually aroused, wants intercourse, and thinks that is what she is asking for as well. Usually the signal is not very clear as to what is really desired on either side.

> The desire to be cuddled and held is acceptable to most people as long as it is regarded as a component part of adult sexuality. The wish to be cuddled and held in a maternal manner is felt to be too childish; to avoid embarrassment or shame, women convert it into the longing to be held by a man as part of an adult activity, sexual intercourse.[5]

It is important, of course, to make sure the signals are clear. That is, healthy males are always immediately sexually aroused if we feel that a woman desires us. That is the way God built and wired us. It was a design by God to guarantee the survival of the human race. It ensured that in primitive society males impregnated their woman regularly and often. If God had not designed this intense and immediate response in men to any gesture of desire on the part of women, men would have wandered off to hunt and fish, forgetting about women and neglecting the perpetuation of the race. In that case, golf would have been invented 50,000 years ago, and the human race would now be extinct. There is today, for example, a direct correlation discernable between the frequency of male golfing and the infrequency of female pregnancy, in the general population. The inverse correlation is equally strong. That, of course, confirms my theory!

When we feel a strong need for sensuous body contact and simple caressing, we must ask for it in a clear and straightforward manner and point out that we are not in this case asking for intercourse. The difficulty with this proposal about clear and forthright signals, however, is that for women at least half of the sense of being cherished is to feel that their husbands, friends, or lovers intuit what they need without having to be told. Well, that is a nice idea, when it works, but it is pretty tricky to get it to work with most males, who happen, just then, to be halfway through the sports page, getting the rundown on the Tigers game, which, of course, they watched strike by strike, from beginning to end, already last night! Moreover, the Bengals lost the damn game as well!

Annamae came to see me because her husband seemed to be more joyful when he was around one of their female friends than when he was around her. Of course, I asked her for as much of her story as she could tell me. She and her husband were both 32 and had been married for 10 years. They had two children, and she thought that they had always worked out a fairly nice arrangement for doing everything together as a family. When I asked her about whether she thought she got most of her gratification and meaning from her relationship with the children rather than from her relationship with her husband, she said that she thought she had always maintained a normal orientation toward him rather than being preoccupied with the kids. Moreover, they both worked full-time, they had had the same daytime nanny for the children since their infancy, and her husband assisted with the care and nurture of the children more than most fathers did.

The family took rather extended and elaborate vacations together at least twice a year and always built them around the children's fun as well as their own. Now that the children were moving from childhood toward pubescence and adolescence, the family's entertainments were moving appropriately to more mature kinds of activity. They were one nice, happy family, except for the fact that she felt something was missing between her and her husband,

Eddy. Annamae had no anxiety about her husband being unfaithful. It was just that he seemed to have so much more fun with her friend than with her. When that friend, Eva, was around, his humor brightened. He seemed more lively and joyful. He would suddenly change from a quiet, pensive guy to a very verbal and expressive conversationalist. She longed for that kind of person in his relating with her.

I asked her to tell me about the other woman. She said that she was attractive, but she did not think the friend was more attractive than Annamae herself. She was not as slim and slender as Annamae correctly thought herself to be. Her friend was a bit chunky. I sensed that Eva had enough "meat on the bones" to emit an aura of fertility. I pointed out to Annamae that because she had insisted on getting herself down to one of those New York–style stick figure shapes, she did not have that same aura about her, and perhaps that could have something to do with the difference in her husband's responses to her and her friend. We talked a while about male visual stimulation and emotional and erotic response to female symbols of fertility. In the end, however, we agreed that this track was probably a dead end street for trying to figure out what was going on inside her husband's psyche.

Because Annamae loved their friend and was not fearful of her husband being really *sexually* distracted toward Eva, it was clear that there was something about the spirit or style of Eva compared with Annamae that was important to Eddy's response. Annamae responded to this notion by saying that Eva laughed easily, was playful, and tended to touch people a lot while talking to them. This was true if Eva was talking to Annamae, to Eva's husband, to the local pastor who was everybody's friend, to Eddy, or to the local drunk who came by begging now and then. I asked Annamae how that compared to her own spirit and style.

She said that she had never been able to be spontaneously humorous or playful. She was especially not at all touching. It always seemed like there was some responsibility to take care of. A child needed attention; the underwear and socks needed to be taken out of the dryer, folded, and put away. A cobweb needed to be wiped off the chandelier, or the table needed to be set for dinner. She admitted when pressed that her husband helped her with at least half or more of these responsibilities, but she often had to point out to him what needed to be done next, and there always seemed to be something.

Moreover, she said that her family was not a touching family like her husband's was. She said, "That family is besotted with each other." Whenever they get together, there is no end to the hugging and kissing and handshaking and patting on the shoulder, and the like. They wash each other with words and physical contact. She said that when she came into the family, all this body contact scared the hell out of her. She had gotten past the point of thinking it was perverted and now saw how normal it is for most folks, but she still had difficulty receiving it and was really unable to respond in that same sensuous and touching way.

Just as I was about to say something to her regarding, therefore, understanding her husband's enjoyment of Eva's expressiveness, Annamae surprised me by saying that she thought the problem was not in her husband but in herself. Then the real story started to unfold. She said that she thought the truth about the whole thing was that she was jealous of Eva for her ability to be so expressive and relate so easily because what Annamae really wanted was to be touched, held, hugged, caressed, fondled, and generally cuddled a lot more than she was. She said she had wanted for years to ask her husband to hold and nurture her with body contact because she had become aware in their marriage that she suffered from an enormous skin hunger. However, she had never been able to put a name on it and, because she did not know what to call it, had never able to tell her husband of her need. She felt shameful about not being able to be spontaneous about body contact and did not know how to get started in the direction of getting her skin hunger fulfilled.

Annamae was also aware of the fact that her skin hunger was the sensuous level of a deeper hunger for frequent lovemaking, sexual play, and real spiritual connection with Eddy. She had always been caught between feelings that such intense desire for sexual play was somehow contrary to being a proper lady, on the one hand, and the feeling that it was really the glorious destiny of a whole-hearted woman, on the other. I proposed to her my idea about life as foreplay and love as the continuing tender cherishing, connectedness, and rich communion of two good lovers. She spontaneously responded that this sounded exactly like what she was trying to express.

She came from a family of a scolding mother and an intimidated father. She resented the fact that her dad had never "stood up" to her negative mother and "told her to shut up and sit down." Annamae felt that she had married a husband who was strong, but also caring, kind, and gentle. She liked that in Eddy. She wished her father had been similar to that. Then he would have been free to be more tender and expressive to her without her mother always getting in the way. As it was, when she began in puberty to blossom as a developing girl and young woman, her mother had mocked her for her growing sexuality and scolded her father about staying away from her. As a result, her father seemed to withdraw from her just when she needed his affirmation and love the most. Just then she really needed his affection and affirmation, so that she could learn to believe that she would be a good and beautiful woman.

As a result, Annamae had no idea how to relate to an adult male in a wholesome sensual and sexual way. So she felt isolated, distant, unaccustomed to body contact, and lacking in spontaneity in relationships. Her weight loss and stick figure body was not so much a result of her trying to conform to the national style of today. It was a result of her never feeling whole enough inside herself to have a normal appetite or the ability to let herself go in freely enjoying any aspect of life. She enjoyed sex with her husband when they engaged in it, but she never initiated it, and could never quite feel the deep connection for which she longed. Annamae thought of herself as having a kind of sickness that kept her lonely and skinny. She wanted very much to change that. I showed her Montague's remark regarding this.

> The mother's holding and cuddling of the child plays a very effective and important role in its subsequent sexual development. A mother who loves must enfold the child she loves. She must draw the child to her in a close embrace and, male or female, this is what the adult will want later and be able to demonstrate to anyone he [or she] loves. Children who have been inadequately held and fondled will suffer, as adolescents and adults, from an affect-hunger for such attention.[6]

Annamae immediately recognized herself in this illumining observation. Her self-diagnosed "sickness" was a vast lack of the healing power of sexuality and sensuality. This derived from an infancy and childhood in which her skin hunger had not been stimulated, and her sexual and sensual selfhood had not been affirmed. She was such a sufficiently healthy and responsible person, nonetheless, that she had managed to have a relatively normal marriage, despite this enormous incapacity for spontaneous body contact.

Many women with the same malady become pregnant in adolescence, not because they wanted sex but because they used sex as a means to get held and caressed. Sexual activity was the price they were willing to pay to get their skin hunger satisfied in some degree. However, the process of the foreplay and afterplay is more important and pleasurable to them than the intercourse itself. Both men and women who have affairs do so for this very same reason. Deficits in the healing power of sensuality and sexuality in their relationships with their spouses make them desperate for someone who will satisfy their outer skin hunger and their inner spiritual longing for real connection.

There is a general myth that is popular in American culture particularly that normal healthy men have midlife crises, and thus when they reach about age 55 or 60, they are driven to attach themselves to younger women, at the expense of their spouses and their marriages. That is most likely a lie in all of the cases, and always a lie in most cases. What would be helpful in each case would be to track down the level of sensuality and sexuality present in their marriages at that time in their lives.

Moreover, it would be useful to determine which of the two spouses prompted the decline in that kind and quality of body contact between them for the decade or two prior to what is now being called the male's midlife crisis. In most cases the person who moved away from the relationship and into a private and isolated world was the woman because of all the reasons we have already discussed. It is not his midlife crisis but hers. Healthy and wholesome males do not want to be unfaithful to their wives, betray their marriages, jeopardize their estates, risk the esteem of their children, or raise questions about their own integrity.

However, they also need good reasons to stay in a relationship, and those reasons include the healing power of sexuality and sensuality that all of us, male and female, absolutely need. We owe it to each other, and each of us has full responsibility for it ourselves. Sensuality that is healing, in this context, means the continuing touching, caressing, tender gentleness, and fondling of the erogenous zones of a lover's body, including genitals, throughout adult life and old age. These are the zones of the body where we have all the most intense nerve endings that are gratifyingly and healingly stimulated by tender touch and that give us profound sensuous and sexual gratification. Healing sexuality in this setting means continuing into later adult life all the techniques that can be gratifyingly arousing and can continue to lead to intercourse, with all of its spiritual benefits, even in very advanced old age.

I have two friends who have now been married for 50 years. They are both beyond the age of 70. They have always had a fairly intense life of sensuousness and sexual play. They tell me that to this day they are both still very sensuous and sexual with each other, to the great gratification of both. Their relationship has not been wholly tranquil along the way. They have both grown a lot over the years and have become much more genial and tender toward each other, but their sensuousness and sexuality have always seemed to heal all the wounds and turbulence that their life together brought their way. She is as intense in her desire for the continuation of their sensuous and sexual life as is he. They tell me that their genital play and tactile stimulation of each other's erogenous zones and skin contact are as intense and pleasurable as they were when they were young. They seem much younger and healthier than their years.

It proved to be quite fortunate in the case of Annamae and Eddy that she was fairly accurate in her assessment of his true nature and character, as well as of her own malady. I urged her to ask him to come to therapy with her so that we could explore what could be done to open the doors of her life to more spontaneous expression and gratification of her skin hunger and longing for a deeper union between them. Eddy was most interested to be involved and do what he could.

Almost as soon as the three of us began to talk about Annamae's feelings concerning her youth, developmental years, relationship to her parents, and experience with Eddy's family, two things happened. First, Eddy was very understanding and intuitive about her struggle. He was tender in his invitation for her to be more risk-taking and fearlessly expressive of her needs and desires. He suggested that he would help her feel safe in giving and receiving sensual and sexual overtures with him. Second, Annamae immediately became less cramped and guarded in her style of expressing and relating with Eddy. The more she verbalized her feelings about her longings, the freer she seemed to be about relating how she had felt all these years, how she now felt, and what she thought she really needed and wanted. Her entire personality seemed to come alive in a new way.

The outcome for this couple was a natural growth in their ways of relating and a rather spontaneous resolution of her impasse. As she felt freer for all sorts of body contact, and he demonstrated that he had always desired that kind of touching spontaneity, they both began to see their relationship as fun rather than responsibility. This sparked an entirely new level of humor and playfulness, a potential that they had not known existed in their marriage. In fact it was the sexual playfulness more than any other specific behavior in the relationship that really healed Annamae. This new level of lightheartedness and joy engaged the children as well. Children are always a good gauge of what is going on in a family. This renewal did not decrease either Eddy's or Annamae's delight in their relationship with Eva, but it enormously increased the delights of their joy in each other and the fun of their family. They were healed by the freeing of the power of their sensual sexuality. They found the deep spirituality in it. Of course, there are now a lot more spider webs around the chandelier.

Ellis made a point of the fact that sexual playfulness is crucial to healing persons and relationships. He claims that playfulness between lovers crafts a relationship that is like creating an object of art.

> It is in this sense that we are here concerned with what we may perhaps call the play-function of sex. As thus understood, the play-function of sex is at once in an inseparable way both physical and psychic. It stimulates to wholesome activity all the complex and inter-related systems of the organism. At the same time it satisfies the most profound emotional impulses, controlling in harmonious poise the various mental instincts. . . . it is certainly true that, in proportion as we truly and wisely exercise the play function of sex, we are at the same time training our personality on the erotic side and acquiring a mastery of the art of love. (81)

Ellis went on to observe that the longer he has lived, the more persuaded he has become of the immense importance of the "development through the play-function of erotic personality," both for individual persons and for the quality of the entire society in learning the art of loving. He found himself astonished that erotic personality is such a rarity and that people are as ignorant as they are of the art of love (81). Although people are good at procreating, he noted, they are not generally very good at making love playfully. He observed mournfully,

At times one feels hopeless at the thought that civilization in this su-premely intimate field of life has yet achieved so little. For until it is gener-ally possible to acquire erotic personality and to master the art of loving, the development of the individual man or woman is marred, the acquire-ment of human happiness, and harmony remains impossible. . . . Lovers in their play—when they have been liberated from the traditions which bound them to the trivial or the gross conception of play in love—are moving amongst the highest human activities, alike of the body and of the soul. They are passing to each other the sacramental chalice of that wine which imparts the deepest joy that men and women can know. They are subtly weaving the invisible cords that bind husband and wife together more truly and more firmly than the priest of any church. And if in the end . . . they attain the climax of free and complete union, then their human play has become one with that divine play of creation in which old poets fabled that, out of the dust of the ground and in his own image, some God of Chaos once created Man[kind]. (82, 87)

Nothing contributes so strongly to our sense of profound wholeness of body, mind, and spirit as do playfulness and sexual intercourse. Healthy women tell me that the arousal of sexual play gives them the sense of being completely OK, completely cherished, and completely their true selves. Women tell me, moreover, that the thrusts of penetration in intercourse with a tender lover give them the feeling of being completely desired and thor-oughly filled and fulfilled. It affords a sense of being completely joined and at one with their lover and at peace with the entire world.

I can testify to a comparable experience as a male, and I find it is typical of healthy, cherishing men. Savoring the loveliness and aura of luxuriant physicality while caressing and exploring a woman's body and then enter-ing her in intercourse, gently, tenderly, excitedly, vigorously, and completely, feels like everything that was ever lacking to my whole self is in that expe-rience fulfilled. As I have said before, it feels like a ship that, having passed through the trying seasons of longing, waiting, and expectation, has finally come home to its haven, a congenial and tranquil harbor of wholeness and peace. It is a blessed homecoming, full of all the meaning I ever needed, a confluence of physical and spiritual fulfillment. Then lying there in the time of afterplay is like rest and recreation in heaven.

There are numerous reasons and kinds of reasons that sensuality, sexual-ity, sexual play, and sexual intercourse have the power to heal our bodies, minds, and spirits. These causes include at least mechanical reasons, chemical reasons, psychological reasons, and spiritual reasons. Let us look at each of them separately and in the order I have suggested here.

First, then, what could be the mechanical reasons that sexual play and the very act of intercourse can be tangibly healing for us at all the levels of our beings? We carry on our daily lives with responsible attention to the duties and opportunities of life. That takes from us a great deal of energy. It induces considerable amounts of tension and perhaps even anxiety. It also depletes us of our reserves of endurance and motivation to drive on.

If at such a point in our day, we have the experience of someone caressing and desiring us, it gives us a new sense of empowerment at the mechanical level. It makes us feel more hopeful and ready to act on the connection with that person. We might simply take the time for some real connection and communion over a Coke or cocktail. Embracing each other by means of good conversation restores our sense that life is a positive pleasure. Holding hands, touching, or actually hugging and caressing gives us an entirely new sense of strength and of the worthwhileness of things.

Should such sensuousness lead on to arousal and intercourse, the mechanical side effects of that bring along a surge of strength. It can give us a fresh sense of well-being that makes the day feel new and at its dawning. In that feeling of joining, penetration fills the woman lover with a sense of fullness and the male with the ultimate sense of completeness. This brings that "one flesh" union, a bond of belonging as one with the other. The very mechanics of this act and process release the muscle tensions built up throughout the day and resolve the sense of the turbulence of things. This quiets the waves of concern life brings, producing a physical state of quiescence, tranquility, and peace.

Sensuous sexuality and intercourse mechanically move our bodies, which have collected the stresses of life, to the rest and release that blesses us with physical health. Old Anna in Schlossmann's clinic healed children by touching and holding them physically. Just so, sexual play and intercourse afford the body contact, the skin-on-skin mechanics, and the stimulation of all those epidermal erogenous cites that restore our entire organism to its fine-tuned normal state. If we were computers, we would say that sex and sensuality are like restoring our entire program to default position. Sexual intercourse and climax are like hitting the restart or restore button. Even at this mechanical level, they incite forces that enhance our health in body, mind, and spirit.

Then there are the chemical forces at play in our sensual stimulation of each other, our sexual play and intercourse. Most people are sufficiently in touch with their bodies and well enough instructed in simple biology to realize that there is a rich panoply of chemical reactions going on inside us all the time. These are particularly active and important in sensuality and sex. We have already rehearsed the fact that our hypothalamus manages the signals that must be sent to our pituitary, instructing it to secrete the necessary chemicals in our bodies to do an enormous number of things. The pituitary controls our thyroid gland, instigates lactation in pregnant or postpartum women, and makes sure of a very lot of other important continuing functions in our total system.

Our thyroid glands are particularly important to our sexual play and grat-ification. The thyroid is the thermostat, so to speak, for about 40 or 50 hor-mones that regulate every thing from digestion to reproduction. A healthy thyroid ensures that we have healthy levels of estrogen, progesterone, testos-terone, adrenaline, and insulin in our bodies. Most of these and many other hormones are directly related to our sexual play and performance. One of the interesting things about the human organism is the fact that a woman may have a number of maladies going on in her chemistry, but when she becomes pregnant, the chemistry associated with pregnancy often fine-tunes her en-tire system in such a way that she does not suffer from those maladies so long as she is pregnant. This is often the case, for example, in women who suffer from a chemistry-based depression. When they are pregnant, they are no longer depressed. Depression returns when the pregnancy chemistry falls off after delivery of the baby. Pregnancy chemistry makes her healthy.

My youngest daughter suffers from multiple sclerosis. She has two daugh-ters who were born sometime after her diagnosis was established. During both of her pregnancies, the symptoms of her MS completely disappeared and returned only after the babies were born. The chemistry of the thyroid-managed endocrine system almost magically arranges the hormone flow so as to compensate for any illness that might exist in the mother to endanger the baby in the womb.

In a very similar manner, the chemistry that is stirred up by sexual play, intercourse, and orgasm fine-tunes our entire systems in such a way as to restore for a time a normalcy in all the facets of our persons. Sexual arousal and the specific stimulations that are produced in the vagina, the mound of Venus, the penis, and the testicles during sexual intercourse normally produce the optimum levels of estrogen, testosterone, and oxytocin neces-sary for a real sense of well-being. Moreover, sexual intercourse produces a strong response in the pancreas and adrenaline glands, resulting in a flood of metabolized sugar to the muscle tissues of our bodies and giving us elevated energy and excitement—a kind of high.

Most important are the chemical reactions produced by increases in blood pressure, heartbeat, rapid breathing, and the heart-lung oxygen exchange. By the intricate chemistry of that process, the entire body is supplied with health-affording levels of oxygen. This is especially true for the genitals, erogenous zones, muscles, and brain. The entire organism is chemically tuned up by the stimulations of intercourse and orgasm. No wonder couples live decades longer than singles. It is just a healthier way to go.

However, that is not all there is to it. The psychological reasons that sexu-ality and sensuality heal us are just as interesting and important. Perhaps they are even more so. I noted in an earlier chapter that Bailey emphasized the importance of the "one flesh" experience. That is the deep, authentic union that sexual play, intercourse, and orgasm bring with them. This is related to the point I have made throughout this book regarding sexual union being the pouring out of ourselves for and into our lovers. Bailey's point is quite interesting. He wants us to notice that for real sexual play and authentic union in intercourse, both lovers need to enter into the experience with irrepressible desire and consent. Only then can we pour ourselves out freely for each other.

To put that simply, it means that sexual play and intercourse are healing if they are the climax of two lovers authentically and freely seeking the gratification of each other. Beginning with a true sense of mutuality, the unfolding sensuality and sexuality can build to a climax. That affords both lovers a sense of completeness and fulfillment. Not every sexual act sets up a valid pouring of ourselves out for our lovers. Healing comes only from those encounters in which there is mutual desire and consent, both for the sexual play and intercourse, and all that follows from it. So, mutual desire and intent are fundamental. It is not just an agreement to perform sexual gymnastics that bonds us. Nor is it a marriage license that unites lovers. It is rather that mutuality that actually makes them a unity in thought, intent, motive, and understanding about what their connection and union amounts to or means.

Psychologically, it is our sense of unity in mind and spirit that makes sexual play and intercourse such a wholesome nurture, feeding our inner tranquility and healing us. Intercourse makes us feel that any isolation, alienation, or loneliness we may have suffered is now so far down the list of important things that it is no longer worthy of serious consideration. We feel one with our lover, one with the universe, and perhaps even one with God. The mechanical release of which I wrote earlier contributes to the sense of psychological release and fine-tuned psychological normalcy as well. This is reinforced by the fact that the chemistry of sexuality and orgasm produces that high, which I mentioned, and floods our bloodstream with oxytocin. This has a direct enhancing effect on the psychological tranquility we feel, and it intensifies our feelings of tenderness, love, and gratitude toward our lover.

Finally, sexual intercourse heals us spiritually. Remember that spirituality is defined, for the purposes of this book, as our irrepressible hunger for meaning in life. Perhaps it is readily obvious, then, what I mean by sensuality and sexuality healing us spiritually. It gives us a profound sense of personal meaning. This includes feelings of the meaningfulness and infinite worthwhileness of most everything in life. No matter what the state of affairs may be in our lives at that moment, they seem secondary to the positive meaning we feel. So the mechanical, chemical, and psychological healing that sexual play and intercourse produce in us directly serves to heal us spiritually. They all contribute to give our entire organism the well-being in which we are sure that life is a delicious process that leads to gratification and joy. It makes the past forgivable and the future desirable, because the present is so full of meaningful wholeness.

If your sense of spirituality is only horizontal in its dimensions, the healing power of sexual play at least affords you the meanings that come from communion and union with a gratifying human lover. If your sense of spirituality is vertical as well as horizontal, it implies that your meaning quest is for God as well as for meaningful relationship with other persons. Then sexual play and intercourse will have an additional dimension of meaning. It will fill your spirit with a sense of the incredible appropriateness of the way God has fashioned and wired the world, particularly the world of interpersonal relationships. It will give you not only the gratification of pouring yourself out for your lover but also the overflowing gratitude to God for his presence to you in the lover with whom you can achieve such life-fulfilling union.

There is so much in loving you
That makes me whole
In body, mind and in my soul
I cannot think how I should live
Without you there to whom to give
Myself in sensual sex for you

You heal me love, as none else can
You make me well
In deeper ways than words can tell
There is no way that I can be
My whole true self except as "We"
God must have had this in his plan

CHAPTER 10

SUMMING UP: SEXUALITY AS A SPIRITUAL WAY OF LIFE

So life lived as foreplay leads to deep experiences of meaningfulness. That achievement requires good attention given constantly to sensual relating and sexual play. That is sexuality as a spiritual way of life. If I were young again, say 20 years or so, and knew then what I know now, I would pursue my life with much more freedom and much more of a conscious and intentional quest for sexual and spiritual meaning. My culture at that time was quite emotionally and sexually constraining. However, I am certain now that my own neurotic anxiety and primitive spirituality were much more constraining than the culture of my conservative Christian society. I think I can now see that my picture of what the culture required was far less humane than that society itself. I grew up with anxiety about and restraint upon my freedom to express my emotions and spiritual insights that was as high as the anxiety I felt upon expressing my sexuality.

Were I young again, and knew then what I know now, I would pursue these matters of my spirituality and sexuality with much more freedom, imagination, and meaning. I would trust God's grace more thoroughly and explore my sexuality with a joyful freedom, if not a sense of abandon. I would take into account the fact that God designed and empowered both my spirituality and my sexuality, that my urges were God's urges expressed in that aspect of this marvelous creation that is me. I would be delighted with the surges of feeling and longing and desire that this incredible gift from God called sexuality afforded me.

I would begin to cultivate early in my exploration the experience of all of life as foreplay. I would be infinitely more sensual and through that find or understand my spirituality, rather than doing it the other way around. I would not again spend decades cultivating a deep sense of spirituality and then try to figure out how to fit my inherent sensuality and sexuality into that in a responsible way. It is possible, you know, to be so heavenly that you are of no earthly good. I would put as much energy into understanding my spirituality but would recognize that my sexuality is a crucial aspect of that very spirituality. There has always been the tendency in the Christian community to emphasize the rubrics and ideals of spirituality as though it is exclusively a transcendent relationship with God, thus blinding us, particularly sensitive children, to the fact that we cannot know God except in our connection with our real inner selves and with others.

Because spirituality is our irrepressible hunger and quest for meaning, we can find it only in gratifying relationship with others or with another. Then we discern the meaning of our relationship with God, as a person, by analogy from what relationship with another *human* person is like. That is why sexuality and spirituality cannot safely be sheared off from one another. In our sexual connections and communion, we discover the deepest and most profound experiences of relationship. It is the projection of that deep profundity upon our connection with God that reveals the true nature and the transcendent dimension of spirituality. That is why we speak of both our ultimate connection with a human lover and our ultimate communion with God as the ultimate sexual and spiritual experience of ecstasy.

In a sound psychology of spirituality, we need to understand how much sexual energy is involved in driving the dynamics of our hunger for God. It shapes our sense of God's presence, our communion with God, and our oneness with God in life. That is, our libido generates strong forces compelling us to long for meaningful connectedness with the transcendent world as much as with the tangible experiences of everyday life. Our longing for illumination from God and for the discernment we derive from human persons comes from our sexual urges for connection with that other.

Our libido is the dynamo in which all those forces are generated that drive us intensely and incessantly toward each other as human companions on the road of sexual and spiritual life. It is precisely in our most intense experiences of sexual union that we have the opportunity to discern the depth of the well of our own spirituality, our hunger for meaning. Our deep spirituality is evident in our discovery, through meaningful sexual union, of how great our capacity is to really cherish another person and truly let the other person into us to cherish us. We find out there and then who we really are.

If I am a man who screws the daylights out of a woman and then turns over and smokes a cigarette, I am a neglectful, insensitive, and isolating fool. I deprive myself of life as foreplay and afterplay, and I make it clear that my union with my "lover" is fake. I have merely masturbated in her, not made love. If I am a woman who entices a man just to confirm to herself the strength of her winsome powers or just to release her masturbatory urges, I am a superficial and trivializing woman, incapable of real relationship. I deprive myself of the opportunity of true sexual and spiritual fulfillment.

In that experience I find nothing of my own spirituality, and I give to my lover no spiritual cherishing or nurture or vision. There is no connection between two lovers in such an experience and hence no connection between the sexuality and spirituality of either. The only meaning that can be in it is the release and relief of libidinal urges. One cannot come away from such a romp with any gratification of the inner hunger for the meaningfulness of life. It offers no whisper of the possibilities of transcendent and eternal ecstasy.

If I were young again, and knew what I know now, I would begin my sexual and spiritual life with a much wider range of exploration. I would try hard to trust my own personal experience in that exploration. I would depend on my own perception of the meaning of my experiences. I would reflect thoughtfully on what illuminations my exploration was giving me about the nature and relationship of my sexuality and spirituality. That is, I would think out as carefully as possible, while I went along the pursuit of that life quest, what it was that I could see as giving genuine meaning to my life and loves.

I would savor the flavor of that meaningfulness in my experience. I would discard and thereafter avoid, in so far as possible, what was in itself meaningless sexual-spiritual experience. I would avoid whatever jeopardized the quality of life and relationship. In this manner I would weigh carefully what it is in my sexual exploration that is truly spiritual, namely, truly meaning-affording. Conversely, I think that in this discernment process I could begin to understand early in life what it is in my spirituality that gives depth and profundity to my sexuality and its expression in union with a lover.

Life is foreplay.
That always dawns on me again
When I touch your arm with grace.
The kindly thought in it
Reminds me that right there
Is the meaning of my life.

Life is foreplay.
That leaps with joy into my mind
As I reach out to kiss you.
The tenderness I feel
Speaks to me more truth
Than teachers can ever tell.

Life is foreplay.
How could I know this in advance?
Though the longing in my soul

Compelled me in the quest
Toward a true heart's hope,
Then far from understood.

Life is foreplay.
I know it now because of you.
In you, my long sought haven,
For body, mind, and soul:
Union and Communion,
An ecstasy from heaven!

Life is foreplay,
For heaven and our other world!
There is our long sought harbor.
Is there a difference
Knowing you, *knowing* God?
Meaning in relationship?

Life is heaven:
Our afterplay is heavenly.
Heaven is our afterplay:
Real life and more the same
Trajectory of love,
Utter union: love's ecstasy!

So let us then sum up the spirituality of sex. We all hunger for fulfillment in body, mind, and spirit. That fulfillment comes through experiences
with each other that give us deep sensations of how full of meaning life is as
we live it. Conscious and intentional cultivation of tenderness and profound
presence to one another leads to contact, connection, communication, and
communion. In this experience, union, ecstasy, and a sense of eternity can
move us beyond the simple mechanics of sex to the spirituality of genuine
and life-giving relationship. That sense of eternity is a transcendence of our
selves and a breath of the eternal and the divine. That is what life can be
every day. We are fortunate to live it.

Series Afterword

The interface between psychology, religion, and spirituality has been of great interest to scholars for a century. In the last three decades a broad popular appetite has developed for books that make practical sense out of the complicated research on these three subjects. Freud had a negative outlook on the relationship between psychology, religion, and spirituality and thought the interaction between them was destructive. He saw sexuality and spirituality as opposing forces and was certain that religion was a delusional projection of sublimated sexual drives. Jung, on the other hand, was quite sure that these three aspects of the human spirit were constructively linked, and one could not be separated from the others. Anton Boisen and Seward Hiltner derived much insight from both Freud and Jung, as well as from Adler and Reik, and fashioned a useful framework for understanding the interface between psychology, religion, spirituality, and human social and sexual development. We are in their debt.

This series of general interest books, so wisely urged by Greenwood Press, and particularly by its acquisitions editors, Suzanne Staszak-Silva and Debbie Carvalko, intends to define the terms and explore the interface of psychology, religion, and spirituality at the operational level of daily human experience. Each volume of the series identifies, analyzes, describes, and evaluates the issues of both popular and professional interest that deal with the psychospiritual factors at play (1) in the way religion takes shape and is expressed, (2) in the way spirituality functions within human persons and shapes both religious formation and religious expression, and (3) in the ways that spirituality is shaped and expressed by religion.

The books in this series are written for the general reader, the local library, and the undergraduate university student. They are also of significant interest to the informed professional persons, particularly in fields somewhat related to religion, spirituality, and social psychology. They have great value for clinical settings and ethical concerns as well. I have spent an entire professional lifetime focused specifically on research into the interface of psychology, sociology, sexuality, religion, and spirituality. These matters are of the highest urgency in human affairs today when religious motivation seems to be playing an increasing role, constructively and destructively, in the arena of social ethics, national politics, and world affairs.

The primary interest in this present volume is in the dramatic and crucial way in which sexuality and spirituality are to be seen as the same vital force in human nature as God designed it. In terms of the field and science of theology and religious studies, this volume investigates the operational dynamics of our spirituality and sexuality as expressions of our quest for meaning in life and in our relationships with each other and with God. This book addresses issues that are of universal concern but at the same time very personal and close to home for each one of us.

Not all of the influences or expressions of human sexuality and its relationship with spirituality throughout Christian history have been inadequate. Indeed, much of the impact of the great religions on human life and culture, including sexual ethics, has been redemptive and generative of great good. It is urgent, therefore, that we discover and understand better what the spiritual, theological, sociological, and psychological forces are that empower people of faith and genuine spirituality to give themselves to all the creative and constructive enterprises that, throughout the centuries, have made of human life the humane, ordered, prosperous, and beautiful experience it can be at its best, in the practice and celebration of spirituality and sexuality. Surely the forces for good in both religion and spirituality far exceed the powers and proclivities toward fear and constraint, or license and promiscuity that we too often see in our world today.

Spirituality and sexuality are part of the essence of being human. They are two expressions of the same inner life force. If one is expressed in a distorted manner, that distorts the other one. When the Medieval mystics repressed and sublimated their sexuality, their spirituality became psychotic. When in our day spirituality is truncated and ignored, sexuality has become insanely irresponsible, shearing off sexual gymnastics from meaningful emotion and relationship. When the central energy of our inherent vitality expresses itself in a transcendent reach for meaning and connection, through our psyches, toward God, we call it spirituality. When that same force expresses itself horizontally through our psyches and bodies toward another human, we call it sexuality. It is the same force. Healthy sexuality and spirituality are inseparable. When either sexuality or spirituality has been suppressed, manipulated, or erroneously controlled as a means of coercion, by the church or other authorities, that has been monstrous and destructive of human wholeness.

This volume demonstrates with numerous detailed illustrations what may be profoundly enhanced in our outlook on sexuality and spirituality so that our delight in these vital facets of our lives and loves may be refurbished, so that we can enjoy the celebrated and wholesome sexuality and spirituality God intends us to experience. This volume is a companion to other recently published Praeger imprints by the same author: *Sex in the Bible, A New Consideration* (2006), *Understanding Religious Experience, What the Bible Says about Spirituality* (2007), and *Radical Grace: How Belief in a Benevolent God Benefits Our Health* (2007). It is also related to an additional volume in this Praeger Series titled *Sexual Liberation, The Scandal of Christendom* (2007), by Raymond J. Lawrence Jr.

J. Harold Ellens

NOTES

FOREWORD

1. Donald Capps (2005), *A Time to Laugh: The Religion of Humor*, New York: Continuum, 110.

2. Stephen Dunn (1994), "Decorum," in *New and Selected Poems*, New York: Norton, 24–25.

3. James B. Naylor (1986), "Authorship," in Russell Baker, ed., *The Norton Book of Light Verse*, New York: Norton, 164.

4. Michael Agnes, ed. (2001), *Webster's New World College Dictionary*, 4th ed., Foster City, CA: IDG Books Worldwide, 1,545.

5. William Stafford (1998), "A Ritual to Read to One Another," in *The Way It Is*, St. Paul, MN: Graywolf Press, 75–76.

CHAPTER 2

1. Maija Jespersen is a teacher of art in a school for mentally and emotionally handicapped children and is a graduate student working toward her PhD in the history, nature, and remedy of sociopolitical violence.

2. Havelock Ellis (1957), *On Life and Sex*, New York: The New American Library–Mentor, 53. (Original publication by *Medical Review of Reviews* in 1921, republished by George Doran Company in 1922 and 1931.)

3. Ibid, 54.

4. Ibid.

5. H. Jackson Brown Jr. (1991), *Life's Little Treasure Book on Marriage and Family*, Nashville: Rutledge Hill Press.

6. Anastasia Toufexis (1993), "The Right Chemistry, Biological and Chemical Factors in Romantic Love," in *Time* 49(3), February 15, pp. 48–51.

7. Dorothy Tennov (1979), *Love and Limerence, The Experience of Being in Love*, New York: Stein and Day.

8. Elizabeth Barrett Browning (1940), "Sonnets from the Portuguese, stanzas XIV and XLIII," in *English Writers*, rev. ed., eds. Tom P. Cross, Reed Smith, Elmer C. Staufer, and Elizabeth Collette, New York: Ginn and Company, 490–491.

9. Robert Browning (1934), "Any Wife to any Husband, Stanzas I and IX," in *The Poems and Plays of Robert Browning*, eds. Bennett Cerf and Donald S. Klopper, New York: The Modern Library, 63, 64.

10. Browning (1955), "Any Wife to Any Husband, Stanzas I and IX.

11. *Romeo and Juliet*, II.1.15.

CHAPTER 3

1. Havelock Ellis (1957), *On Life and Sex*, New York: New American Library–Mentor, 53.

2. I Kings 10 and II Chronicles 9.

3. This presentation of the narrative of the Song of Songs was first published in J. Harold Ellens (2006), *Sex in the Bible, A New Consideration*, Westport, CT: Praeger, and is used here by permission. The text is Ellens's translation of the original biblical Hebrew text.

4. T. P. Cross, R. Smith, E. C. Stauffer, and E. Collette (1940), *English Writers*, New York: Ginn, 154.

5. William Shakespeare, Sonnet 43.

CHAPTER 4

1. Robert L. Moore (1992), "Decoding the Diamond Body: The Structure of the Deep Masculine and the Forms of Libido," in Fredrica R. Halligan and John J. Shea, eds. *The Fires of Desire, Erotic Energies and the Spiritual Quest*, New York: Crossroads.

2. Marie M. Fortune (1995), *Love Does No Harm: Sexual Ethics for the Rest of Us*, New York: Continuum.

3. James B. Nelson (1995), introduction to *Love Does No Harm: Sexual Ethics for the Rest of Us*, by Marie M. Fortune, New York: Continuum, 11–12.

CHAPTER 5

1. Thomas Merton (1955), *No Man Is an Island*, New York: Harcourt Brace–Dell, 26. Merton was a monk in the Abbey of Our Lady of Gethsemani in New York. He is most famous for his work *The Seven Storey Mountain*.

2. Ibid.

3. Ibid.

4. Truman Esau and Beverly Burch (1990), *Making Marriage Work, Developing Intimacy with the One You Love*, Wheaton, IL: Scripture Press–Victor, 41–42.

5. Ibid., 49–50.

6. Jerry Greenwald (1974), *Be the Person You Were Meant to Be*, New York: Simon and Schuster.

7. Greenwald (1975), *Creative Intimacy, How to Break the Patterns That Poison Your Relationships*, New York: Simon and Schuster.

8. Ibid., 156.

9. Raymond J. Lawrence Jr. (1989), *The Poisoning of Eros, Sexual Values in Conflict*, New York: Augustine Moore Press.

10. Raymond J. Lawrence Jr. (2007), *Sexual Liberation, The Scandal of Christendom*, Westport, CT: Praeger.

CHAPTER 6

1. Theodor Reik (1945), *Psychology of Sex Relations*, New York: Grove Press, 194.

2. Leslie Karen Lobell (2000–2006), http://www.eNotalone.com/article/1117.html, *Not Alone—Sex and Romance—Orgasm*.

3. Ibid.

4. Julian Jaynes (1976), *The Origin of Consciousness in the Breakdown of the Bicameral Mind*, Boston: Houghton Mifflin.

5. On this point, see Nelson S. T. Thayer (1985), *Spirituality and Pastoral Care*, Philadelphia: Fortress, 88.

6. Ibid., 28.

7. Henri J. Nouwen (1979), *The Wounded Healer: Ministry in Contemporary Society*, New York: Image.

8. Nowen (1969), *Intimacy*, San Francisco: Harper and Row, 23.

9. Ibid., 36.

10. Ibid., 29.

11. Ibid., 29, 36–37.

12. Ibid., 29.

13. Ibid., 31–32.

14. Ibid., 33.

15. This is the author's own translation of I Corinthians 13:4–8, on the model of that of J. B. Phillips (1958), *The New Testament in Modern English*, London: William Collins Sons and Co. LTD and Geoffrey Bless LTD.

16. Derrick Sherwin Bailey (1952), *The Mystery of Love and Marriage, A Study in the Theology of Sexual Relation*, New York: Harper and Brothers, 65.

17. Thomas Moore (1994), *Soul Mates, Honoring the Mysteries of Love and Relationship*, New York: HarperCollins, xvii.

18. Ibid., 96.

19. Ibid., 98.

CHAPTER 7

1. Alexander Lowen (1965), *Love and Orgasm, A Revolutionary Guide to Sexual Fulfillment*, New York: Macmillan–Collier.

2. Ibid., 11.

3. Ibid.

4. Ibid., 12.

5. Ibid., 12–13.

6. Ibid., 15.

7. Eric Fromm (1956), *The Art of Loving*, New York: Harper and Row, 28. See the comment on this work of Fromm in Alexander Lowen (1956), *Love and Orgasm, A Revolutionary Guide to Sexual Fulfillment*, 28.

8. Robert K. Johnson (1989), *Ecstasy, Understanding the Psychology of Joy*, San Francisco: Harper and Row, vi–vii.

9. For further explication of the contrasting sets of ideas in this paragraph, see Johnson, ibid., 115–32.

CHAPTER 8

1. Ashley Montague (1971), *Touching, The Human Significance of the Skin*, New York: Columbia University Press.

2. Ibid., 1.

3. Dante Gabriel Rosetti (1872), "The Kiss," in *The House of Life*, in *Poems*, 6th ed., London: Ellis.

4. J. Lionel Taylor (1921), *The Stages of Human Life*, New York: Macmillan, 157.

5. Montague, ibid., 94.

6. Judith C. Lechman (1987), *The Spirituality of Gentleness*, San Francisco: Harper and Row, 42.

7. Howard H. Brinton and Margaret Hope Bacon (1964), *Friends for 300 Years: The History and Beliefs of the Society of Friends Since George Fox Started the Quaker Movement*, Wallingford, PA: Pendle Hill Publications, 68.

CHAPTER 9

1. Anna Freud (1965), *Normality and Pathology in Childhood*, New York: International Universities Press, 199.

2. Ibid.

3. Ibid.

4. Ashley Montague (1971), *Touching, The Human Significance of the Skin*, New York: Columbia University Press, 189.

5. M. H. Hollender, L. Luborsky, and T. J. Scaramella (1969), *Body and Sexual Excitement, Archives of General Psychiatry*, Vol. 20, 218; see also Hollender (1970), "The Wish to Be Held," *Archives of General Psychiatry*, Vol. 22, 445–53.

6. Montague, ibid., 188.

BIBLIOGRAPHY

Bailey, Derrick Sherwin (1952). *The Mystery of Love and Marriage, A Study in the Theology of Sexual Relation*. New York: Harper and Brothers.

Brinton, Howard H., and Margaret Hope Bacon (1964). *Friends for 300 Years: The History and Beliefs of the Society of Friends Since George Fox Started the Quaker Movement*. Wallingford, PA: Pendle Hill Publications.

Browning, Elizabeth Barrett (1940). "Sonnets from the Portuguese, stanzas XIV and XLIII," in *English Writers*, rev. ed. edited by Tom P. Cross, Reed Smith, Elmer C. Staufer, and Elizabeth Collette, 490–91. New York: Ginn and Company.

Browning, Robert (1934). "Any Wife to any Husband, Stanzas I and IX," in *The Poems and Plays of Robert Browning*, edited by Bennett Cerf and Donald S. Klopper, 63, 64. New York: The Modern Library.

Cross, T. P., R. Smith, E. C. Stauffer, and E. Collette (1940). *English Writers*. New York: Ginn.

Esau, Truman, and Beverly Burch (1990). *Making Marriage Work, Developing Intimacy with the One You Love*. Wheaton, IL: Scripture Press–Victor.

Fortune, Marie M. (1995). *Love Does No Harm: Sexual Ethics for the Rest of Us*. New York: Continuum.

Freud, Anna (1965). *Normality and Pathology in Childhood*. New York: International Universities Press.

Greenwald, Jerry (1974). *Be the Person You Were Meant to Be*. New York: Simon and Schuster.

Greenwald, Jerry (1975). *Creative Intimacy, How to Break the Patterns That Poison Your Relationships*. New York: Simon and Schuster.

Halligan, Fredrica R., and John J. Shea, eds. (1992). *The Fires of Desire, Erotic Energies and the Spiritual Quest*. New York: Crossroads.

Hollender, M. H. (1970). "The Wish to Be Held." *Archives of General Psychiatry*, Vol. 22.

Hollender, M. H., L. Luborsky, and T. J. Scaramella (1969). "Body and Sexual Excitement." *Archives of General Psychiatry*, Vol. 20.

Jaynes, Julian (1976). *The Origin of Consciousness in the Breakdown of the Bicameral Mind.* Boston: Houghton Mifflin.

Jespersen, Maija (2008). Personal correspondence.

Johnson, Robert K. (1989). *Ecstasy, Understanding the Psychology of Joy.* San Francisco: Harper and Row.

Lawrence, Raymond J., Jr. (1989). *The Poisoning of Eros, Sexual Values in Conflict.* New York: Augustine Moore Press.

Lawrence, Raymond J., Jr. (2007). *Sexual Liberation, The Scandal of Christendom.* Westport, CT: Praeger.

Lechman, Judith C. (1987). *The Spirituality of Gentleness.* San Francisco: Harper and Row.

Lobell, Leslie Karen (2000–2006). *Not Alone—Sex and Romance—Orgasm.* http://www.eNotalone.com/article/1117.html.

Lowen, Alexander (1965). *Love and Orgasm, A Revolutionary Guide to Sexual Fulfillment.* New York: Macmillan–Collier.

Merton, Thomas (1955). *No Man Is an Island.* New York: Harcourt Brace–Dell.

Montague, Ashley (1971). *Touching, The Human Significance of the Skin.* New York: Columbia University Press.

Moore, Robert L. (1992). "Decoding the Diamond Body: The Structure of the Deep Masculine and the Forms of Libido." In Fredrica R. Halligan and John J. Shea, eds., *The Fires of Desire, Erotic Energies and the Spiritual Quest.* New York: Crossroads.

Moore, Thomas (1994). *Soul Mates, Honoring the Mysteries of Love and Relationship.* New York: HarperCollins.

Nouwen, Henri J. (1969). *Intimacy.* San Francisco: Harper and Row.

Nouwen, Henri J. (1979). *The Wounded Healer: Ministry in Contemporary Society.* New York: Image.

Phillips, J. B. (1958). *The New Testament in Modern English.* London: William Collins Sons and Co. LTD and Geoffrey Bless LTD.

Rosetti, Dante Gabriel (1872). "The Kiss." In *The House of Life*, in *Poems*, 6th ed. London: Ellis.

Shakespeare, William. *Romeo and Juliet*, II.1.15.

Shakespeare, William. Sonnet 43.

Taylor, J. Lionel (1921). *The Stages of Human Life.* New York: Macmillan.

Tennov, Dorothy (1979). *Love and Limerence, The Experience of Being in Love.* New York: Stein and Day.

Thayer, Nelson S. T. (1985). *Spirituality and Pastoral Care.* Philadelphia: Fortress.

Toufexis, Anastasia (1993). "The Right Chemistry, Biological and Chemical Factors in Romantic Love," in *Time* 49(3), February 15.

Index

About the Author

J. HAROLD ELLENS is a retired university professor of philosophy and psychology, a retired US Army Colonel, a retired Presbyterian pastor and theologian, Executive Director Emeritus of the Christian Association for Psychological Studies International; Founder and Editor in Chief Emeritus of the Journal of Psychology and Christianity, a clinical psychotherapist in private practice, the author, co-author, or editor of 175 volumes and author of 166 professional journal articles. He continues in his role as Adjunct Professor of Philosophy and Biblical Studies at University of Detroit Mercy, in Classics at Wayne State University, and Research Scholar in the Department of Near Eastern Studies at the University of Michigan. His books with Praeger include *Sex in the Bible*, *Radical Grace*, and others.

About the Foreword Author

DONALD CAPPS, PHD, is the William Harte Felmeth Professor of Pastoral Psychology at Princeton Theological Seminary, where he has been a faculty member since 1981. In 1989 he was awarded an honorary doctorate from the University of Uppsala, Sweden, and he served as president of the Society for the Scientific Study of Religion from 1990 to 1992. His books include *The Child's Song: The Religious Abuse of Children* (1995); *Men, Religion, and Melancholia: James, Otto, Jung and Erikson* (1997); *Jesus: A Psychobiography* (2000); *Freud and Freudians on Religion: A Reader* (2001); *Young Clergy: A Biographical-Development Study* (2005); *Fragile Connections: Memoirs of Mental Illness for Pastoral Care Professionals* (2005); *A Time to Laugh: The Religion of Humor* (2005); and *Jesus the Village Psychiatrist* (2007).